TIME LTD

Transform your busyness into a thriving business

Steven Watson

To Sacha,
 Thanks for your rebellious
  support!

FISHER KING PUBLISHING

Steven

TIME LTD

Published by
Fisher King Publishing
The Old Barn
York Road
Thirsk
YO7 3AD
England
www.fisherkingpublishing.co.uk

Edited by Jo Watson
www.agoodwriteup.com

Cover design by Definition Consulting
www.definitionconsulting.co.uk

Dedicated to *'my girls'*

Mum, who taught me how precious time really is.
I miss you.

Jo, who I always want to share every moment with.
I love you.

And Lily, who I could never have too much time with.
I'm proud of you.

Contents

Foreword

There are only two problems with time.

Firstly, there isn't enough of it.

Secondly, anything you do to free-up time doesn't seem to work. You try it. It might or might not work for a while. But you never stick to it – slipping back into old ways, eventually.

In fact, there's a common misconception about time – 'There isn't enough of it... and there's nothing that can be done about that.'

This isn't true, of course.

Some people are massively efficient. They always get stuff done. They don't procrastinate. They achieve lots each day. After reading this book... you'll be that person. You'll get a lot MORE done in a lot LESS time.

In this book, Steve's come up with some clever techniques and ideas to help you find more time to achieve what you want and need in your business. And, more critically, he shows us how to embed these new techniques, so that they become our habits.

This is life-changing stuff. If you can save an hour per week, that's 50(ish) hours per year – which is one whole working week! That's a holiday!

Save 2-3 hours a week, and you've saved 2-3 weeks per year. Weeks you'd probably have spent in boring meetings or engaged in other stuff you just don't need to do. As I say... life-changing.

My advice? Get some paper, a pen and a cuppa. As you read and learn, write down everything in this book that will save you time. And then, implement it straight away.

(I have a response ready for you if you tell me you don't have the time!)

I know lots of people who've followed Steve's techniques in business. Those techniques work, and you're about to save yourself weeks every year.

Andy Bounds

Award-winning sales consultant, best-selling author and creator of www.andyboundsonline.com

Start with time

Time is everything, and everything starts with time.

Whatever you want in your life, whether you achieve it or not will largely depend on what you do with the time you have. Whether you want better mental and physical health, more quality time with your family, or to build an organisation that will be your legacy, it's a pretty safe bet that it requires you to make good use of your time.

By picking up this book, you have taken the first step towards Time Mastery. Time is your most important resource, and so learning to make the most of it is not only the first step to your success, but *every* step to your success.

This book aims to 'Transform your Busyness into a Thriving Business', so let's clarify that with a couple of definitions.

'**Busyness**': *The feeling of being active all day, every day, regardless of productivity.*

'**Thriving Business**': *An effective use of time that provides you with exactly what you want in your life.*

It's time to stop wishing that you could make *more* time and commit to start making ***more of*** the time you already have. Time is everything. The way you invest yours will determine the way you can spend your life.

How will this book help you?

I sincerely hope this book will inspire you to master your time and transform your busyness into a thriving business, as the title and cover suggest.

A common theme throughout this book is 'time habits'. That's because around half of what you do on a day-to-day basis is habitual, rather than deliberate. If you can develop effective time habits in your life, it will represent a big step forwards in your pursuit of time mastery.

There is a lot of behavioural science behind the approaches used to develop time habits, but you won't read a lot of detail on that in this book. It's designed to be a book of action, rather than one of theory. Essentially, time habit development is based on these three things:

1. A 'Gimme Five' streak

There is a lot of evidence to say that if you want to make something into a habit, it needs to be really simple to do initially. Gimme Five is something you can do for just five minutes to get you started. It's subtly very powerful, because although there's the opportunity to stop after those allocated five minutes, you'll probably find that when you have beaten that initial procrastination and made a start, you will usually want to continue long after the set period has passed. When you carry out that simple task for the second day in a row, you are on a 'streak', and when you maintain a streak for enough consecutive days... it becomes a habit.

That may seem like an overly simplistic view of habit formation, but it's true. There are tons of reports and studies about the time it takes to form new habits, but the truth is that it depends on so many things, and so it's pretty much impossible to put a universal timescale on habit formation. For simplicity, all you really need to know is that if you repeat an action enough times, it *will* eventually become a habit.

2. When and Then

Attaching desired actions to existing behaviours is very powerful. The trick is finding the most effective behaviours to attach those desired actions to, and a tool I use to do this is called 'When and Then'. Maybe you want to make time to check your schedule for the day every morning. If so, maybe you can attach it to boiling the kettle for your morning cup of coffee. '*When* you boil the kettle, *Then* you check your schedule'. If you get distracted regularly, you can make it a habit to do something about it. '*When* you get distracted, *Then* write down what distracted you and put something in place to make it less likely to happen again'.

If you have a tendency to over commit... '*When* you are asked for a completion date, *Then* delay giving an exact time until later'. People are usually happy for you to do this if you explain that you don't want to commit to anything you can't deliver, and promise to let them know later that day. It gives you enough breathing space to make a rational decision about what you can realistically do, after the excitement of wanting to impress or 'win' the business has died down a bit.

3. Rewards

There are many ways of rewarding behaviour that you want more of. During the process of developing a time habit it is advisable to mark and reward every successful repetition in a small but meaningful way. Using the calendar on your phone to update your current 'streak days' tally so that you can see the progress you've made is a good start, and if you tell someone else where you're up to, that's even better.

If you use Gimme Five Streaking, When and Then, and Rewards, you'll be giving yourself the best possible chance to develop the time habits that will help you on your way to mastering your time. Make sure you keep the focus on quality over quantity. The more habits you try to develop at once will split your focus between them, which can decrease the effectiveness of each one. I would recommend having only one or two new time habits under development at any one time.

Inspiration

Reading books and listening to audiobooks is undoubtedly the Time Habit that has helped me to develop the most in my personal and professional life. In days gone by, that would probably be as far as your relationship with the author would go, but it's easier than ever to connect with people these days thanks to the digital world we live in. When I'm inspired by someone's work I often try to connect with the creator of it. As a result, I have been able to speak to a lot of fantastic people over the years, and at each time, I have learned to ask them a powerful question:

'Who inspires you?'

I'd recommend you start asking the same.

When you look into what inspired the people who inspire you, it's very inspiring. And that's a lot of inspiration! I have taken some book titles from authors that have personally inspired me in my life and in my work, and have created playful variations of them as headings and titles throughout this book. I did this mainly as a nod of acknowledgement and gratitude, and also a fun way of sharing some of my inspiration with you. I wonder how many of the titles you will recognise.

Speak to people who inspire you, and ask them who their inspirations are.

Where to start?

It's probably a fair assumption that you didn't pick up this book because you have too much time on your hands and nothing to do with it.

I don't want you to be tempted, in that case, to just dip in and out of it when you can grab 5 minutes here or there. You can certainly do this if you need a refresher on anything, or you need a bit of instant insight, but ideally, I want you to work through each of the stages (blocks) in order.

You don't have to do it all in one go, of course, but everything's been written in a short, sweet and simple fashion that would certainly allow you to do that.

There is beauty in simplicity, and this book is full of simple ideas presented in a simple way. So, if you read something that seems *really* obvious, just ask yourself honestly, 'Do I actually do this, though?'

In my experience, when things get complicated, we often forget to do simple things that contribute to our success. Things like having breakfast, exercising and allowing ourselves to switch off and fully recover.

Busyness causes us to be overwhelmed and stressed, and when that happens we often can't see the wood for the trees, as they say.

Whilst nothing fully eradicates stress (and that's actually a good thing), Time Mastery certainly gets rid of that sense of overwhelm. This book starts with The Pyramid of Time Mastery, which acts as your guide to the content on this journey and also the map to mastering your time.

Let's get started.

The Pyramid of Time Mastery

There is no shortage of advice out there about time management. In fact, the last time I Googled the term, it produced over four and a half billion results. With so much information out there for us to so easily access, it would be fair to question why people are still struggling with their time, don't you think?

My take on it is that the quantity of information far outweighs the quality, and there is a lack of structure in how to apply it. The structure that's needed, I believe, is a pyramid.

There are a lot of factors that contribute to Time Mastery, and this structure is the simple method I have created to identify them, explain how they are interrelated, and show how they can systematically be developed. It's called the Pyramid of Time Mastery.

The Pyramid of Time Mastery

Understanding the pyramid

The base of the pyramid is the foundation that everything else is built on, and if it isn't strong, the whole thing will crumble. For that reason, we need to make sure that the key blocks in the foundations of your pyramid are strong.

LEVEL ONE - THE FOUNDATIONS

Why: If your *why* is strong enough, the *how* becomes a formality. You can't expect yourself to put a lot of effort into something if you don't have sufficient motivation to do it. Simon Sinek's excellent book advocates that you should 'Start with Why'. This section of *this* book will help you to understand your true purpose and the reasons for what you do, and will let them fuel your passion to achieve whatever you set out to do.

Awareness: In order to improve at anything, you need to have an understanding of your current position. You need to know what you're doing well and where you can improve. Self-perceptions can often be biased as people often view themselves how they *want* to be seen rather than how they actually are. For that reason, the MOT (Mastery of Time) Test in this section of the book is a really useful tool for making you more aware of your current use of time.

Vision: Without a clear vision of where you want to go, it's impossible to plan a route to get there, Steve Jobs said, "If you are working on something exciting that you really care about, you don't have to be pushed. The vision pulls you". Your vision is much more than just a dream. It is something that you can see and believe, and you really feel that you can achieve it. What does your vision for your future look like? Let's get clear on that.

Planning: Armed with a clear vision, you need to plan how you are going to achieve it. Your vision may be a long way from your current situation, and as such, it could seem quite intimidating to think about. You could be forgiven for wondering how you will manage to achieve it, but when you break it down into manageable chunks, you can concentrate on the process of what you need to be doing at any given moment rather than overwhelming yourself with thoughts of the final outcome and everything that contributes to it all at the same time. Think of it as you would with any physical journey. Most of the time, you can't see the final destination when you first set off. You just look for particular milestones and act accordingly. You may join a specific road, turn right at a junction, and take a certain exit from a roundabout. You don't tend to worry too much about anything other than the next milestone. You can do the same with your vision. In this section, you will break your vision into milestones so that you can stay focused on simply moving towards the next one.

Mindset: Dr Carol Dweck's psychological research explains the difference between a fixed mindset belief (that talents and abilities are innate and unchangeable), and a growth mindset belief (that you can get better at anything if you commit attention and energy to it). It's important to think with a growth mindset if you want to improve your time mastery. For example, you may hear people say they are 'always late', as if it is a permanent character trait. It's essential to adopt a mindset that allows that statement to change to something more desirable, such as, 'I'm working on my timekeeping'. This section encourages you to think about time in a different way by shifting the focus from problems to solutions.

LEVEL TWO - THE SKILLS

With Why, Awareness, Vision, Planning and Mindset in place, you can move to the second level of the Pyramid and build on it with the next four blocks.

Productivity: This is one of the better-known phrases you'll recognise in the Pyramid, and it's all about your ability to get things done efficiently. This section has plenty of tips for that.

Being productive builds on the solid foundations below it and turns all of the motivation and preparation into the ability to get things done in a timely way.

Organisation: Even with the best intentions in the world, it is likely that you will forget about things and double-book yourself if you are not organised enough with your time. Equally, if you don't manage projects effectively, you'll forever be struggling with deadlines and performing far below your potential. Whether managing a project, your team's time, or your own day, 'scheduling time to schedule your time' is incredibly powerful, and doing it will be a huge step in the right direction for you on your time mastery journey. You'll have more tools to help you become more organised after reading this section.

Discipline: Doing what you say you are going to do, even long after the mood you said it in has disappeared, is something we can all be guilty of falling short with. Being held accountable for those things in an effective way will make sure that you are disciplined in your approach to time. Without discipline, you will never be able to stick to things you know you need to do on a consistent basis. Things will come up, people will distract you, and sometimes you simply won't feel like doing what you need to do. At times like these you will need discipline, and that's what this section is all about.

The 3 Cs – Clarity, Communication, Consistency: Whether you are trying to motivate your team, explain why people should work with you, or set expectations with your clients, effective communication skills are essential. Of all the organisations I've had the good fortune to work with, the most successful ones have consistently had the most clarity and the best communication. This section provides you with some helpful hints to improve your 3Cs.

Once these blocks are in place you can move up to the next level of the Pyramid, where you will see a big shift in your relationship with time.

LEVEL THREE - APPLICATION

Strength: When faced with difficulties, your strength, experience and resilience give you the capacity to recover quickly and respond in a way that allows you to keep thriving. You are probably going to experience challenges in some form on a daily basis in your business, so you need to be in the best position possible to survive and thrive in the face of them. This section prepares you for dealing with some of the biggest challenges you are likely to face.

Balance: Taking its place at the centre of the pyramid to ensure everything is weighted, is balance, and this is all about keeping on top of your relationships, mental health and physical health as well as your work. Too often, you see people doing really well in one area of their life, but it's to the detriment of other key areas. Having the right balance in your life is essential if you are to experience the happiness and benefits of time mastery. There are tips in this section for getting that balance right.

Habits: A large portion of the things you do on a day-to-day basis are habitual. They are the things that happen automatically without you thinking much (if at all) about them, such as your relationship with the snooze button, how you take your morning coffee, and the radio station you listen to when you click on that button. This section will help you to develop productive and much 'healthier' habits that will free up time, help you avoid time stealing mistakes, and set you up for success.

With Strength, Balance and Habits all in alignment, you will be in a good position to progress to the next level.

LEVEL FOUR – THE BENEFITS

Autonomy: Life can get overwhelming when you have lots of things to do that you don't actually have much control over, but by this stage you should be able to build on the other elements of the Pyramid to feel more in control of your time and your life. To have autonomy in your life is to largely be able to do *what* you choose, *how* you choose, *when* you choose.

Influence: Feeling in control of your own time is a massive step in the right direction when it comes to time mastery, and it is greatly enhanced by an ability to influence the people around you. The preceding blocks in the pyramid all contribute to your ability to encourage others to respect your time - and be more productive themselves at the same time. With Autonomy and Influence, you are in a very strong position to move up to the top of The Pyramid of Time Mastery.

LEVEL FIVE - THE PINNACLE

Freedom: When people are asked about their ultimate goal in life, they will often allude to having lots of money and plenty of time; and the desire to spend both of those things however they want. Essentially, what they want is freedom. When you have achieved the financial freedom of no longer needing to work, along with the desired balance that you want in your life, it's pretty safe to say that you have mastered your time.

Imagine what this will look like for you. By starting with the end in mind like this, you can create a vivid vision of what you want - and a roadmap for making it a reality.

What will time mastery mean for you?

Where are you starting from?

Which foundations are already solid for you?

Dig out your spade, grab your high vis vest, and reach for your hard hat – we've got a pyramid to build!

It's time to get to work on laying those foundations!

Level One

Block 1

Why

Your why is your purpose

When you know your *why*, everything you do has purpose. The fog of confusion lifts and you can see in high definition where you are going. It's clear what you need to prioritise and easy to let go of everything else.

Lots of people are unsure of their purpose, and this is often clear to see by the way they act. They jump from one thing to another as if they are frantically searching for the idea that will be 'The One' to bring them success. Is that you?

Conversely, it is very easy to see when someone is crystal clear about their purpose and what they are trying to achieve. They are focused on their goals and have the burning desire to do whatever is needed to reach them. They never veer off that track.

That's the reason that clarifying your 'why' is so important. Everyone *has* a why, but some people need help *identifying* it.

Lots of people will tell you that their family are their 'why', but despite being incredibly important motivators for you, they are not the type of answer we are looking for in this instance. Maybe don't tell them that!

For the purposes of this exercise, your 'why' is something very personal about who you are as a person. It's a common theme that runs throughout everything you do and is likely to be something process-based like teaching others or giving people a voice, rather than outcome-based like having a big house or providing for your family.

If you can't identify your 'why' by yourself, it can be useful to have a conversation with someone to help you find it. By asking enough questions about someone, you can identify common themes that may start to make sense in the search for a person's why. If you want to do this for yourself, consider choosing a few of the following questions as inspiration:

- What do you spend most of your time thinking about?

- When you last woke up feeling really motivated, what did you have planned for the day ahead?

- Why do other people need what you're best at?

- If you had a free day, how would you spend it?

- How do you think people who know you the best would describe you?

- How would you *like* them to describe you?

If you haven't worked it out yet, take the time to get clear on your 'why'. Look inside yourself for the things that you love doing, and look *outside* of yourself to recognise the impact those things have on the world when you do them.

Any questions?

It's pretty standard to ask this at the end of a presentation, meeting or conversation, but unfortunately, by that time it can be too late.

Imagine you spend ages explaining something you feel is important or interesting, but all that time your audience is wishing you were talking about something else.

It's normally useful to know what the question is before you give the answer, isn't it? That's why, in preparation for this book, I sent a message to a random selection of people I know in business, to ask them the specific question, "What are your biggest time challenges right now?" They knew I was writing a book and that this is why I asked, but I've changed the names anyway:

Claire says she's always busy and loads herself up with stuff to do, but that seems to be the very thing that stops her from actually doing it.

Emma struggles to identify what to prioritise. She doesn't like to let people down so tries to do everything, and that causes her a lot of stress.

Alex is a self-confessed procrastinator, especially when he is working from home. There are so many distractions and it's hard for him to ignore them.

Jen just wants to put the chaos in her mind into some kind of order so that she can manage her time – and her life - better.

Ian wants to find the balance of reducing stress levels but still making sure he gets things done.

None of these came as a shock, because we've all felt like we've been in these scenarios at some point, haven't we?

This book addresses all of the above scenarios and challenges with time - and more besides. I sincerely hope you find the answers that you are looking for in the coming pages.

What is the true cost of poor time management?

You already know that time is the most precious thing you have. You know that unlike money, once time is spent there is no way of getting it back. You know that you're older and wiser than you've ever been - but also younger than you'll ever be again.

But yet, even with this knowledge, you still waste time every single day. That's a shame, isn't it? Actually, it's a tragedy.

Let's consider the true cost of poor time management in a hypothetical scenario:

You have your weekly meeting with your team. The agenda is very relaxed and everyone has the chance to get things off their chest. The meeting lasts for at least an hour each time – because that's the way it's always been in your planning. There are 6 people in attendance.

Consider the average hourly rate for each of the attendees. Time spent in that meeting is time not spent doing their job. That doesn't even include travel or prep time.

And then, the meeting over-runs. It always over-runs. This then ends in frustration for at least some of the team. Oh, and don't forget to factor in the cost of the room, the coffees, the resources...

The late finish means everyone is late, frustrated and less prepared than they'd hope for their following appointments – something that snowballs throughout the day, thus adding to the frustration. All of this shows, of course, and you end up losing customers and damaging relationships.

The lost customers mean the company falls short of its targets, and so any hopes of bonuses or pay rises is gone. Morale sinks and pressure rises. Nobody wants redundancies, so everyone works late to make up the shortfall.

You have another meeting to address all of the issues that have occurred. An hour and a half this time. Stress is mounting, and more and more mistakes start to creep in. Customers are leaving and employees are now actively looking for other jobs.

You're home late. Again. And, after a frosty reception, your partner utters those dreaded words... "we need to talk". So, you stay up late, arguing about how you are always stressed and how you don't have enough quality time with the kids. You don't sleep well that night and are tired in the morning.

Stressed, worried and drained, you make poor decisions at work that day. Things are getting worse, and as you arrive home late again, your partner suggests marriage counselling. Along with the financial and time costs of the sessions, it's just another thing on your plate that you could really do without. Your heart was never really in the sessions, and so they don't work.

You start talking about divorce.

Who gets the kids?

You'll have to sell the house.

Everything that happens at home takes your attention further and further away from work.

With more issues to address, and more shortfalls to make up, the weekly meetings are getting longer, more hostile, and less productive. You never get to the gym anymore and your diet is basically takeaways. Stress levels are through the roof and your remaining relationships are crumbling around you.

Everything is going wrong.

And where did it all go wrong?

In this case, it was that weekly meeting.

OK, so this has been a fictional tale and is obviously played out in the worst of worst-case scenarios over a period of time, but sadly, it's not really that unbelievable, is it? It is easy to see how poor time management can snowball into big problems across all areas of your life.

Don't worry, it doesn't have to all be doom and gloom.

What are the true opportunities of good time management?

As well as making some changes to our time mastery – addressing the blocks in the Pyramid, of course – not only can we stop these costs from occurring and spiralling, but we can also open up some opportunities, too!

Let's revisit that team meeting, shall we?

The weekly meeting is coming up, and you have a clear agenda in place, focused on the key drivers of success towards the goals of the business. It's sent out at least 24hrs before the meeting so that everyone can be prepared. That way, the meeting can be more about making considered decisions than about having discussions.

You understand that every meeting carries a cost, so you are very careful to ensure that the meetings only last as long as they need to, rather than blocking out an hour for it because (all together now) it's the way you've always done it. This time it's going to take less than half an hour, so you set the meeting time to 09:00 until 09:27.

Some parts of the meeting are not relevant to everyone, so you cover everything that concerns John early in the meeting and allow him to leave at 09:10. Everything that concerns Danielle is towards the end of the meeting so you tell her she only needs to arrive at 09:15. You decide to hold this meeting virtually so that travel time can be minimised for everyone.

You respect everyone's time and everyone follows your example. The meeting runs to time and the desired outcomes are achieved.

Everyone leaves the meeting with clarity and focus. You go into your next meeting relaxed, prepared and confident. You secure a great deal with a customer that takes the business to its target.

Everyone is delighted. You call home and share the great news with your partner.

Hearing of the success of your business, more customers start to enquire about working with you. The whole office is booming with a sense of pride and achievement. You grow the team and free up plenty of time for yourself to get to the gym and take care of yourself.

You promise your kids that every day you'll get home in time to eat with them and play with them before bed. Your partner is delighted to have you back in the family team.

It's hard to imagine how you could be happier. You are doing well at work, feeling fit and healthy, and your relationships are thriving.

Not a bad life, hey?

The snowball effect

It's amazing how things can snowball. Whether positively or negatively, once momentum builds, the results can be staggering. The determining factor lies in which hill you push the snowball down.

Every choice you make has consequences.

You might think that something as simple as having an agenda in a meeting is insignificant. Trust me, it isn't. Little things like agendas all contribute to the way you manage your time, and the way you manage your time is the way you manage your life.

The Da Vinci road

When Leonardo Da Vinci started to paint the Mona Lisa in the early 1500s, he had a clear vision of what he wanted to achieve. You are no doubt familiar with the outcome of that piece of work. It's sitting in the Louvre hundreds of years later and valued at over half a billion pounds.

Chances are that you are not a professional artist, but try to imagine the process of creating such a masterpiece.

With the first strokes of oil applied to the canvas by our friend, Leonardo, he was setting the foundations that would slowly develop into something wonderful. I can't imagine that he raced through the whole thing like a caricature artist on the Prom at Blackpool.

Da Vinci will surely have given careful consideration and care to every stage of his painting. I imagine he would regularly step back and take a look at what he'd created, see it from a different perspective and make any adjustments he saw necessary. He'd probably look at it one day and see one thing, and then come back the next day and notice something completely different.

Perhaps he also asked for a second opinion at times.

How does it look?

Are there any obvious problems?

What little tweaks can I make?

Sometimes, you can be so focused on something that you can't see it properly. You are so close to a project that you miss things that seem obvious to someone else, and so for that reason, another perspective can be very helpful. Whether or not you take the opinions of others on board is your prerogative, but if you have the opportunity to get some external feedback, you should take it. It's like a mystery prize in a competition. It might turn out to be a load of useless rubbish, but there is always the chance it could be the thing you really need at that moment.

Having waited patiently for months, I wonder if poor Mona asked the question, "Is it ready yet, Mr Da Vinci?". The thought probably crossed her mind, but I doubt she actually said anything. Maybe she knew that the final result would be worth the wait.

It is thought that Da Vinci worked on the Mona Lisa intermittently, adding layers at various times over the years. I wonder if that was deliberate, or whether he was distracted by other things. He was only human, after all!

The Mona Lisa was Da Vinci's masterpiece; the result of the way he spent his time.

What will be the result of how you spend *your* time? It doesn't have to be a painting (and it probably isn't). It might be something tangible you create, or something intangible that makes a positive difference to yourself or the lives of others. Whatever it is, make it your masterpiece.

Money trees and time seeds

"Money doesn't grow on trees!", the parent declares to their demanding child. "If you want it, you're gonna have to earn it!"

Of course, they're correct. Money doesn't grow on trees. But if it did, you'd be planting money tree seeds everywhere you could, wouldn't you?

You've probably also heard people say that time is money. I disagree. Time is time, and money is money. Turning time into money is a skill in itself, and in any case, time is worth far more than money.

I remember seeing my little girl taking her first steps (or sprints, in her case). It might sound a little bit cliché, but it is literally one of those moments in life that I will never forget.

Has there been a similar time in your life, where something wonderful happened without warning? You couldn't have planned it. You just had to be there.

Okay, so how much would you sell that moment for?

Of course, the answer is that you wouldn't sell it because it's priceless.

What about a time or event that you wish you were there for but you missed it. How much would you have paid to be there? I wish I could've been with my mum to hold her hand and comfort her as she fell asleep for the final time. You can't put a price on some things.

Getting back to the title of this section, if you had a chance to plant a seed that could grow into something wonderful, you would undoubtedly plant as many of those seeds as you could and give them all the sun, water and nurturing they needed.

This book is full of time seeds; ideas that can create time for you. Plant them and see what they grow into. If you plant enough, then some will flourish and give you the time you want and need – to do with whatever you like.

Maybe you'll spend more time doing things you *want* to do instead of things you *have* to do, or maybe you'll invest that time and create a money tree after all.

Don't lose any sleep over the seeds in this book that don't grow! If you find just a few things that really help you to make more of your time, it will make the book more than worth the financial investment of purchasing it and the time taken to read it. That's how I see it, anyway – with any book that I purchase myself.

Level One

Block 2

Awareness

Your MOT Test

When your car outgrows its infancy, you take it for an MOT Test each year to check it is fit for purpose and operating in the most efficient way. I think it's about time you started checking yourself in a similar way.

Now, I'm not talking about the medical or health related MOTs that you may be signed up for, so I won't be helping you check your treads, rev your engine, or play around with your dipstick. Instead, I'm going to suggest that you complete a **Mastery of Time** Test. The best way to do this is online at my website, www.27andahalf.co.uk, because as well as being a lot quicker (and isn't that what we want?), once you've completed it, it automatically generates a report of your results! This report highlights not only your strengths but also your areas for development in your relationship with time. There's a manual version of the test in this chapter, too, but seriously – get online.

Most time management programmes start with a requirement to track your time and account for every single thing that you do for a couple of weeks. There is no doubt the value you would get from having that information is huge. In fact, a key reason that people struggle with their time is that they don't understand enough about where they spend it.

One example to illustrate this involves your screen time stats on your smart phone. They tell you exactly how long you've spent on every application, along with your call time and also your 'pick-ups' (when you just flick the screen up to check for activity). Most people are surprised at the results, and frankly, we're *all* a little embarrassed about what the stats tell us about how much of our time we waste every day.

If you don't measure it, you can't manage it.

So, in an ideal world, having an in-depth two-week tracker of information about how you spend your time would undoubtedly be of value. Then again, so would the ability to make an extra few hours magically appear every day. Unfortunately, though, some things just aren't going to happen.

I'm sure you'll agree that collecting such information would be a big ask for someone who was probably drawn to a book like this because they are struggling to achieve all of the things they already need to do in the limited time they already have. Saddling you up with a task like that is probably not the best approach.

You'll be glad to know I'm not going to ask you to track everything you do for a fortnight. But I am going to strongly advise that you complete the MOT Test. It will give you a really good insight into your current use of time, and action points to improve it immediately.

Have a go. Go to www.27andahalf.co.uk and complete the test online. It only takes a few minutes (of course) and provides you with a detailed report about your strengths and areas for development, based on you selecting the answer that most accurately reflects your time habits in response to each question. If you want a sneak peek at the questions prior to logging on, here they are...

1. **Drive – Your why**

    a. I am crystal clear about why I do what I do and I am motivated by it every day (4 points)

    b. I know what is important to me but sometimes I still don't do all that I need to do (2 points)

    c. I don't really know why I do what I do (0 points)

2. Vision – What you want your life to be like

a. I have a written vivid vision of what I want my life to look like in the future (4 points)

b. I have a good idea in my head of what I want to achieve (2 points)

c. I don't really have a clear vision of what I want in the future (0 points)

3. Vision – How it all fits together

a. I have a written vivid vision of the role I want my work to play in my future (4 points)

b. I think I know what role I want my work to play in my future (2 points)

c. I am not sure where I want my work to fit in my future (0 points)

4. Planning – The stepping-stones to success

a. I have broken down my vision into a clear, written plan of realistic milestones and the dates I need to achieve them by (4 points)

b. I have a pretty good idea in my mind of what I need to do to achieve my goals (2 points)

c. I don't really have a clear plan of how I'll achieve my vision (0 points)

5. Planning – The detail

a. The milestones in my plan are VSMART - Visible, Specific, Measurable, Achievable, Relevant and Time-bound (4 points)

b. The milestones in my plan have some VSMART elements, but not all (2 points)

c. The milestones in my plan do not have many – or any – VSMART elements (0 points)

6. Mindset – How you view things

a. I believe I can improve on any aspect of my time management if I set my mind to it (4 points)

b. I believe I have control over my ability to change some aspects of my time management (2 points)

c. I am good at certain aspects of time management but not others, and there isn't much I can do about it (0 points)

7. Mindset – Positive optimism

a. I am very optimistic about my ability to master my time and achieve my vision (4 points)

b. I am fairly positive but also realistic that things may not work out (2 points)

c. To be honest, I am sceptical about my ability to master my time and achieve my vision (0 points)

8. Organisation – Making time

a. I schedule time to schedule my time every day (4 points)

b. I take time to review my schedule every now and again (2 points)

c. What schedule? (0 points)

9. Organisation - Scheduling tools

a. I use an e-calendar to organise my time on a daily basis (4 points)

b. I use a paper diary (2 points)

c. I use a to-do list but not any kind of diary or calendar (0 points)

10. Organisation – Prioritising tasks

a. I prioritise tasks effectively, even when I have loads of things to do (4 points)

b. I am fairly good at prioritisation, but when something unexpected comes up it can throw me off track (2 points)

c. I struggle to prioritise tasks (0 points)

11. Discipline – Doing what you need to do

a. I am very disciplined. I stay productive but never take on more than I can manage. I pretty much always achieve everything I set out to do in a day (4 points)

b. I am fairly disciplined, and more often than not I achieve everything I set out to do in a day, but I sometimes take on too much (2 points)

c. I struggle with discipline, and often find myself overbooked and stressed! I rarely achieve everything I set out to in a day (0 points)

12. Discipline – Accountabilibuddies!

a. I have carefully selected people to hold me accountable for each milestone I need to achieve (4 points)

b. I have someone who holds me accountable to some of the things I need to do (2 points)

c. I don't have anyone holding me accountable for what I need to do (0 points)

13. Productivity - Technology

a. I use technology to my advantage on a daily basis for getting organised, staying focused and being productive (4 points)

b. I find that technology can be both helpful and harmful to my productivity (2 points)

c. I mostly find technology to be harmful to my productivity (0 points)

14. Productivity – Time hacks

a. I have a selection of proven ways to free up time quickly when I need to (4 points)

b. I have a few ideas that might free up some time for me at certain points (2 points)

c. I have no idea how to free up my time (0 points)

15. Productivity – Multi-tasking

a. I consciously avoid multi-tasking (4 points)

b. I sometimes multi-task when I have multiple things to do (2 points)

c. I multi-task every day (0 points)

16. 3 Cs - Selecting the right communication method

a. I am always careful to select the most appropriate method of communication (4 points)

b. I sometimes consider the best method, but often go back to my *preferred* method of communication for everything (2 points)

c. I always communicate using the same method (0 points)

17. 3Cs – Clarity in meeting agendas

a. When I am invited to a meeting I only attend if there is an agenda and it is clear how and why I am required to contribute (4 points)

b. Most of the meetings I attend have a structured agenda (2 points)

c. I attend a lot of meetings that are unstructured (0 point)

18. 3Cs – Consistency with emails

a. My emails serve me on my terms. They do not rule me and never interrupt what I am doing (4 points)

b. My email notifications are off but I check them a lot during the day anyway (2 points)

c. I always have my emails open with new message alerts (0 points)

19. Strength – Dealing with distractions

a. When unexpected challenges arise they very rarely have a big impact on my day (4 points)

b. Sometimes things come up and change my day, but I adapt and cope the best I can with it (2 points)

c. I am regularly distracted and it prevents me from completing what I need to do (0 points)

20. Strength – Saying No

a. I feel confident saying No in an assertive and kind way - and do so regularly (4 points)

b. I don't like saying No, but I do it to protect my time when I need to (2 points)

c. I find it really hard to say No to people when they ask me to do something (0 points)

21. Strength – Beating procrastination

a. I have strategies in place to prevent procrastination (4 points)

b. I do procrastinate at times, but I can get over it quickly (2 points)

c. I am really bad for procrastinating (0 points)

22. Balance – Home time

a. I have set times that I start and finish work and I never work outside of them (4 points)

b. I have a rough time that I finish work and usually stick to it (2 points)

c. I finish at various times, often working very long hours and coming home late (0 points)

23. Balance – Health and Relationships

a. I would rate my mental health, my physical health and the quality of my relationships with family, friends and colleagues as 9/10 or better (4 points)

b. I would rate each of these areas as 7/10 or better (2 points)

c. I would rate at least one of these areas of my life as less than 7/10 (0 points)

24. Time habits – The things you do routinely

a. I have good time habits and am always actively developing new ones (4 points)

b. I have some good time habits that help me to be productive and some not so good ones that don't! (2 points)

c. Most of the time habits I have are not very helpful to my productivity (0 points)

25. Influence – Affecting the behaviour of others

a. I am able to influence others to respect my time and be

productive themselves (4 points)

b. I can sometimes have an impact on how other people treat my time and their own time (2 points)

c. I don't feel as though what I do has any impact on anyone else's time management (0 points)

Although you now have the gist of the questions, statements and weightings involved to get your MOT 'score', it's ideal for you to complete the test online so that all findings can be presented and explained regarding your personal areas of strength and development. The detailed report created for you within seconds of completing the test online will be packed with useful information regarding what you personally need to do to improve your score and therefore take the necessary steps towards time mastery in the future.

Your score:	Date:
%	

By answering the MOT questions, you will have considered things that you may not have done ordinarily, and hopefully gained more clarity over how you spend your time. If you want some additional validation of your answers, go through the questions with someone you have an appropriate relationship and sense of trust with, and listen to their opinions about how they would answer each question on your behalf. This is designed to be helpful, not confrontational, so select that person wisely!

You can talk about any differences in your opinions and then decide whether you want to amend your answers or stick with your original thoughts.

"Did I pass the test?"

There is no 'pass' score. Your total score simply allows you to take a snapshot of your overall time management and give you the opportunity to revisit the test in a few months and monitor your own progress.

Treat your MOT Test as you would with your car's MOT. Put it in your calendar for a few months' time so that you remember to do it (again). Keep records so that you can refer back to and monitor your progress when you want to.

Armed with the information your MOT Test gives you, you can identify your biggest opportunities for development and start to take immediate action.

By combining your test with the Pyramid of Time Mastery, you'll be able to refer to the relevant sections in the contents of this book and quickly jump to the most relevant chapters to meet your development priority. As mentioned previously, though, it's better to go through the book in order to ensure your foundations are solid before building on them with the next blocks.

Remember, this test is not a competition with anyone but yourself. Now is not a time for excuses - it's a time for taking responsibility. Only by being brutally honest with yourself will you be able to identify the best action to take.

Here are five tips for you on self-assessment:

- Measure yourself. Give yourself every opportunity to monitor your progress
- Be honest. Who are you kidding if you're not?
- Compete with yourself. Set the date for your next test and challenge yourself to beat your previous/best score
- Analyse your results. Identify your biggest opportunities for improvement
- Reward your achievements. It doesn't have to be something mas-

sive. If it's meaningful it will reinforce the positive improvement you have made.

The gap

Take a few moments to consider the following questions, based on your MOT Test results:

What are your time management strengths and areas for development?

What is the area for improvement that would make the biggest impact on your time management at this moment in time?

Those answers should give you an initial area to prioritise. You can continue reading the book in its intended order if you want to, or you may prefer to find the relevant section in the contents if there is a particular aspect you want help with straight away. Never forget about the importance of foundations, however.

Whether you are staying here or jumping to another section of the book, try taking these 3 actions to give your productivity a boost before you continue:

1. Identify something that you currently do but is probably a waste of your time. Stop doing it.
2. Identify something that you think is a good use of your time. Do more of it.
3. Try something new that you think might take you closer to your goals. Assess it, and see which of points 1 or 2 it fits into.

Admittedly, this is not mind-blowing stuff I'm telling you here, but the most obvious advice is usually the most effective. Ironically, the most obvious advice is also very often the most overlooked and ignored.

Information-based decision making

Doctors need to diagnose what is wrong with a patient before they can treat them. Addiction meetings require people to accept their current situation before they can move on. Accountants need to know what you're currently spending before they can advise you how to save more money. Addressing time habits is no different. Just as you would do when addressing any other habit in life, you first need to have a good understanding of what you currently do/where you currently are and commit to changing it for the better.

Sometimes it can be beneficial to make decisions based on what 'feels right', but more often than not, decisions based on information and evidence are more effective.

You will be faced with decisions to make on a regular basis in your business, including things like:

- How much to charge
- How long to allocate to tasks
- Which resources need to be deployed
- Which opportunities to pursue

When you make business decisions without sufficient information, the answer you arrive at can vary depending on how you feel in the moment – and how pressured you were to make it.

It's worth collecting data about your work wherever you can. If you know how long a particular job takes you on average - and how much money you make from it - you can make consistent, informed decisions, and also analyse your performance to identify areas for continuous improvement.

You may think working out an average is pointless for jobs that can have such a big variance, but that is what averages are for. They take into account the extremes at both sides and find a figure that summarises the situation. Needless to say, the larger the sample size the more useful the average.

> Self-awareness is essential if you are going
> to successfully master your time.

If you haven't completed the MOT Test yet, continuing to read the next chapters of this book may well feel like searching for treasure in a sunken ship. You may be able to find what you want by just going in the direction that your gut tells you to, but it will be much quicker and easier if you can see where you are going, and in this case the answers from your MOT Test will light the way for you to focus on exactly what you need.

Give yourself the best possible chance of success and complete the MOT Test online now at www.27andahalf.co.uk.

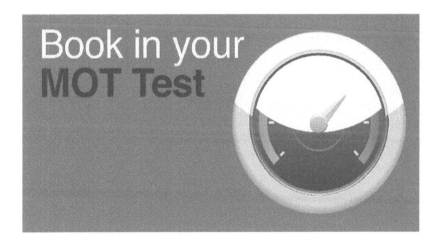

> When you wonder where your time is going...
> Then take the MOT Test.

You should now have a better idea of how effectively you are currently using your time. By reflecting on each section, you will also be able to identify some strengths and areas for development.

Armed with a clear purpose and self-awareness, you are now ready to create a vision of what you want to achieve by mastering your time.

Level One

Block 3

Vision

When asked to create a vision of what you want in the future, it is easy to think about tangible things that you would like to have.

So, instead of what you'd like to *have*, I'd like you to consider what you would like to *be*. That is the great thing about success. More than what you achieve, your real success will be what you become in the process of achieving it.

Raising your business

Are you an 'if you want something doing properly, do it yourself' kind of person? Lots of people are, particularly in their own business.

They treat their business like their baby, and much like a parent, they often enjoy the fact that their baby depends on them. But as babies grow up, they need to make friends, go to school, and generally start to become more and more independent from their parents.

Some businesses never grow up, and there's nothing actually wrong with that. I talk a lot in this book about having a 'thriving business', but this does not necessarily mean a *big* business. A thriving business is one that allows use of your time that affords you the life that you want.

In fact, in many business cases, there's a good argument to say, "Don't try to do more - try to do less!"

However, if you *do* want to grow your business you will probably need to release your grip on its hand and allow other people to contribute to its growth and development at some point.

That doesn't mean compromising quality. Quite the opposite, in fact. If you can surround yourself with brilliant people, it can only strengthen things. These people can be employees, if you like, but they don't have to be. You can outsource a lot of things these days, and when it's done effectively to the right people who can offer the right skill and support, it can make your business more sustainable and scalable in the process. In practice, it's just a mindset shift from doing everything yourself to making sure things are done by the most suitable person.

As the saying goes, "Turnover is vanity, profit is sanity". Being busy is not in itself something to be proud of - but efficiency is. 'Busyness' takes up all of your time, but efficiency gets you to the final result in the quickest time possible.

How long can you hold your breath?

An interesting consideration for you and your business is how long you could last with your current level of expenditure and no more money coming in. In other words, how long can you hold your breath?

Whatever your current capacity, it's a good idea to be aware of it so that you can make informed decisions about your expenditure, and also develop an extra layer of security in case you were to have a few bad months at any point.

Over time, you can look to increase your capacity to survive for longer if there was no more money coming in.

Value, not price

When you speak to your prospective clients in your business, talk about what the results of your work are *worth* rather than an hourly rate for delivering them. Don't keep your results a secret – share stories of the problems you have solved for other people and what impact they have had. By doing this, the proof you offer means you can charge more. Doing that will therefore help you achieve your financial targets more efficiently by needing less clients and, therefore, less time.

It's very often true what they say: Less is more!

So, you'd like to master your time.

Why?

- To have more time for the things you love?
- To reduce stress and take back control of your life?
- To make you more successful?

We'd all like these things, wouldn't we? Success is a strange concept though, isn't it? We can define 'thriving business' as *'An effective use of time that provides you with exactly what you want in your life,'* but what does that really mean?

What does success look like?

I like to network quite a bit as I find it to be a good way of building relationships with people who I'd like to do business with in some capacity either now or in the future. It's a strategy that I use to help me to get closer to achieving my goals, so needless to say, if there comes a time that networking no longer contributes efficiently to that use of time, I'll stop doing it.

It's always surprised me how many people are unclear about what they actually want to achieve when it comes to things like networking. They will attend a session (or any other business activity for that matter) and then make a decision straight away whether it is 'working' or not, without knowing what they were actually hoping to achieve in the first place (never mind giving it enough time to develop into anything).

There's one thing for sure, if you don't know what it is that you are trying to achieve, you'll never know whether you've achieved it or not. That's why it is so important to set a clear vision.

Time to dream...

What is success to you? Take a few moments to get a clear picture of what success means to you. Don't worry about how to achieve it at this point. Just get a clear picture in your mind of what you would want to achieve if you could literally have anything in the world that you wanted.

Can you picture it? If not, go back and try again. If you need inspiration, think beyond physical items and consider what your relationships, your health and your business would look like.

It's great to dream. You may think there's no point in thinking about things you may never achieve, but it's a great starting point for creating a vision.

Turning the dream into a vision

OK, now it's time to bring things back to reality a little bit. Having big dreams is great, but what we are looking for now is a vivid vision that you can believe in and aim for. So, if you dreamed of something like world domination or invincibility, we may need to rein you in a bit!

Think about what you would like to achieve. You can be as ambitious as you like but make sure it is believable, in your own mind at least. A good example of something seemingly wild but not unthinkable involves the Hollywood actor, Jim Carrey. In 1985, as a struggling actor, he had no money at all, but he wrote himself a $10million cheque for "acting services rendered", dated November 23, 1995. He kept the cheque in his wallet. There weren't many people who would've thought he would achieve it, but the reason this is more realistic than it seems is because Jim knew he was a talented actor, and he also knew that the industry he was in could potentially enable him to achieve his vision given his abilities and niche. As you probably already know if you're a film fan, by the time 1995 came around, Jim had starred as the lead role in three Hollywood hits, with the 1994 classic, 'Dumb and Dumber', netting him that cool 10 million in one fell swoop.

If Jim hadn't been a good actor (yes, I know it's subjective), that cheque would've been a dream. Equally, if you are a 45-year-old man you could dream of being a World Cup winning footballer, but it is highly unlikely to happen given the fact that 99% of professional footballers have usually long retired by that point. Your dreams have endless possibilities, but your vision is something you can believe in that will drive you to be the best version of yourself and achieve your potential.

If you were at your very best and could achieve your full potential, what would that look like?

I don't know about you, but if I try to describe my vision in a single word it would be 'freedom', and whenever I've spoken to other people about their vision, theirs always seems to include an element of freedom as well. Broadly, it is often having the freedom to do the things you want to do, when you want to do them, and that usually involves being healthy, having great relationships, and making enough money to be able to afford the lifestyle you want.

When you've got a vivid vision in your mind, get it on paper. You can put it into words or draw it - whatever works best for you. Just know that getting it down on paper confirms it and (almost) brings it to life.

Remember, it's more about what you want to *be* than what you want to have. Now let's get to work on making that vision into a reality.

Level One

Block 4

Planning

You may find it overwhelming to think about how you will be able to achieve your vision. That's natural. It's the reason we are going to break it down into milestones so that you have mini-goals that don't seem too difficult to achieve at all.

Imagine you're crossing a wide river. Jumping across the whole thing seems impossible, but if you have stepping-stones to follow, you can easily make progress towards the other side, one step at a time.

Driving goals

Do you ever drive anywhere without using a Sat Nav of some sort these days? OK, so maybe you don't use it for every journey, but I bet you do when you are going somewhere further than you've been before that takes you a little bit outside your comfort zone.

Why wouldn't you? It takes the destination you want to arrive at and provides you with a simple step by step guide to get there.

It's not so easy when you don't know the address and postcode, however. You could just follow the roads that you think are heading the right way, but chances are that it would take you a very long time to arrive - if you ever got there at all. I mean, how would you know if you'd actually arrived?

Similarly, if you don't know what you want to achieve in life or in business, how on earth will you ever achieve it?

Have a clear idea where you want to go

The beauty of a Sat Nav is that once you've entered the postcode, the technology takes care of the rest. Not only does it map out the best route to your goals, but it also monitors where you are at any given moment in time, to check you're on the right tracks. Then, if any unexpected problems arise, it recalculates the best route for you to follow from that point. Throughout the journey, it will only tell you the next action you need to take, rather than overwhelming you with too much information all at once.

Imagine if it gave you all the instructions all at once. It would be distracting, overwhelming and very unhelpful!

When you're trying to plan any journey, it's always useful to break the big goal into smaller milestones. Start with the ultimate goal, and then work backwards like this:

If you wanted to pass your driving test in 6 months' time (yes, I'm sticking with driving), what stage will you need to be at in 5 months' time?

Where will you need to be – and what will you need to be doing – in order to get to that end point every month from now?

What will you need to have done by the end of today?

With your target date set (let's go for NYE), it's time to look into what you need to do to achieve your goal:

By December 31st

- Get provisional licence, complete approximately 15 practical lessons, practice for around 50 hours out of lessons, gain confidence to drive independently, revise for theory test, book theory test, take theory test, book driving test... take driving test.

That looks like a daunting list, doesn't it, but let's see how it looks when it's broken down into milestones - complete with specific dates that will need to be adhered to in order to achieve your goal on time.

- Apply for Provisional licence by July 1st
- Book lessons and have the first one by August 1st

- Complete 5 Lessons and be practicing twice a week by September 1st
- Theory revision 25% complete, and manoeuvres 1 and 2 mastered by September 15th
- Complete 10 lessons and be practicing independently twice a week by September 30th
- Theory revision 50% complete, and manoeuvre 3 mastered by October 1st
- Theory revision 75% complete, theory test booked, and manoeuvre 4 mastered by October 15th
- Complete 15 lessons, be practicing independently twice a week, and theory revision 100% complete by October 31st
- Theory test passed and practical test booked by November 1st
- Driving test passed by December 31st (hopefully this is enough time to practice and re-book should you fail the first time – apparently all the best drivers do...)

The above information is not designed to be 100% accurate for learning to drive. It's just an example to show how you can break a large project down into milestones so that it seems a lot more achievable. You can use the same principle for any project. Once you've planned everything out and made the necessary preparations, all you really need to think about is putting one foot in front of the other and reaching the next milestone.

Thinking back to that first driving lesson, there seemed to be quite a lot to think about all at once, didn't there?

It's easy to feel overwhelmed with so much going on, but this is a good moment for you to remember that with the guidance of your instructor it all became easier, and eventually you learned to do all of those things on your list without much stress.

You are living and working in a world where everything is moving so quickly, and once again you find yourself with what seems like an unmanageable amount of stuff to do.

- Deadlines
- Meetings
- Incoming calls/emails
- Admin
- Accounting
- Social media
- Personal stuff

There are a lot of similarities between learning to drive and mastering your time. One key difference, though, is that you aren't legally permitted to drive unless you pass a standardised test, but there's no formal test for competently managing your own time.

If you just started to drive without learning, it would cause a lot of harm. It would be madness.

We have already considered the true cost of poor time management, and *that* causes a lot of harm as well. When you are running your own business and your time management is poor, it's usually the most important things in life that suffer.

Honestly, regardless of whether it is the brakes on your car or the things that maintain your health and relationships in life, if you start to forget about them you need to pop the 'L' plates back on before you do some irreparable damage.

One tip that my driving instructor gave to me was to repeatedly "look far, near, rear".

'Far' to see what to expect further up the road.

'Near' to overcome any immediate obstacles.

'Rear' to check what is happening behind you.

I think this is a good thing to do in life outside of driving, too:

Look 'far' to remind you of the goal you are heading towards.

It's so easy to be distracted by the things that are happening right now that you can lose focus of what you're aiming for. You need to constantly remind yourself of your 'why' and the vision you are aiming for.

Look 'near' to make sure you are doing what you need to in order to hit today's milestone. This comes from clarity when scheduling your day. Not only clarity of what you are doing and when, but also clarity of how it fits into the bigger picture. You may find yourself with a meeting in your calendar that you are unclear about the value of. A good way to stay focused is to ask yourself, *"Will doing this take me closer to my vision?"*. If the answer is yes, do it now and do it well. If the answer is no, get rid of it if you possibly can!

Look to the 'rear' to remind yourself of how far you've come and give yourself positive encouragement. When imposter syndrome rears its ugly head, and I think it does for everyone from time to time, you need some reassurance that you are on the right tracks. By thinking about where you started and the obstacles you have overcome on your journey so far, you can get the confidence to push on.

If you are wondering how on earth you will find the time to work towards your vision, you may be tempted to wish you had more time...

More, more, more?

Humans are designed to always want more, regardless of their current situation. Whether it's space at home, money to spend, or time to relax, we always want more of it. No matter much we have and how much we get, it somehow never feels like it's enough.

I think we can establish by this point in the book that you'd like more time, but what do you think you would do if you had it?

- build your business?

- live a healthier lifestyle?

- commit to some learning and development?

- strengthen your relationships?

- enjoy yourself?

Sadly, in reality, it doesn't usually work out the way you think it will when you get what you want. How many times do you hear of people who win the lottery only to find that it didn't bring them the happiness they thought it would? There are countless stories of people feeling 'lost' as they don't need to work anymore, and their relationships with friends and family have been strained as a result.

In a similar way, there is a misconception that simply having more time would be the answer to our problems, but this is rarely the case, because there is an important difference between resource and resourcefulness.

Resource is what you *have*, and resourcefulness is what you *do* with what you have.

Having more resources is not the answer to a lack of resourcefulness. In most cases, it will only serve to emphasise your lack of resourcefulness.

As a result, when hoarders find more space, they usually fill it with more things. When people who are poor at saving get more money, they tend to spend more money. When procrastinators get more... you can guess the rest.

So, we all want more, and that will never change. Thankfully, there are lots of ways to free up more time in your week, but it is worth keeping in mind that having more time is less than half of the solution. How you use it will be the biggest determining factor in whether it makes a difference to your life or not.

I identify all of this falling into one of two camps – time hacks, and time habits.

Time hacks - the things you can do right now to free up some time.

Time habits - the things that determine what you do with the time you have.

There are plenty of each of these things coming up in the rest of the book.

Let's get planning

Don't worry about what other people will think about your goals. Big or small, they're yours - and you need to own them.

So often, people are affected by what other people tell them that they should want. Social media is rife with this because, at its very nature it is a filtered showreel of what people think success is – and what they want you to see. If an 'influencer' says you should get up at 3am, people will do it. If they show you pictures of a Lamborghini in front of a mansion, some people will consider that to be a sign of happiness (possibly the only sign). And if someone tells you that you need to achieve a certain turnover in a week/ month/ year, it can really make you believe that is the benchmark for success.

Your goals are your goals, and nobody else has the right to judge them. Theodore Roosevelt had it right when he said, "comparison is the thief of joy". The problem comes when people are unclear about what their own goals actually are, and it leaves a void that your mind will subconsciously fill by making you look at what others have and compare it to your own situation.

Please do yourself a favour and don't be sucked in by it. Be clear about who you are, what you want in your life, and how you are going to achieve it. If social media didn't exist, this would be what you'd have to do anyway!

Get V.SMART

You've probably heard of SMART goals, but if you haven't, this is what the acronym means: There are various different versions of the acronym, but the basic idea is that if you make your goals Specific, Measurable, Actionable, Realistic and Time-bound, you are much more likely to achieve them.

It is quite common to make the SMART acronym into SMARTER by adding Evaluated and Reviewed. I can get on board with that, but would actually suggest making it V.SMART instead, by making the goal Visible and having people hold you accountable to it.

KISS

Here's another acronym to help you make your plan. KISS. It stands for 'Keep It Simple, Stupid!'. The last thing you need right now is to feel overwhelmed, so don't try to do loads of things all at once. Choose one simple thing as your goal and create a plan to achieve it. If you can't narrow it down to one thing that's ok, but be aware that the more things you are aiming for, the more your focus is divided. Try to keep it simple.

I apologise for calling you stupid, by the way – I promise it wasn't me who created this acronym!

The beauty of breaking it down

One of the key benefits of breaking goals down is the ability to assess whether your plan is worthwhile in the timescale given. If you realise that you would need to be able to achieve far more today than you're capable of, you probably need to reassess the timescales and details and amend the plan accordingly. You need to have a realistic plan that you believe in, and if it isn't quite right on the first attempt, it's better to find out at this point rather than in 12 months' time when you are stressed out because you haven't achieved your goal.

Take the time to plan it, assess it, and rework it until you are happy with your plan.

By breaking things down in this way, it is clear what you need to do right now to achieve your goals further down the line. This is very motivational and can help you to overcome the procrastination of getting started.

You can break your day down even further into 'sprints', if you like. We will talk more about this later in the book, but for now, planning your goals in this way will help you to keep your outcome in mind and also be very clear about the process you need to follow to get there.

Level One

Block 5

Mindset

Wherever you look, you can find an excuse not to do what you should be doing.

The weather.

The government.

Your customer is being unreasonable.

Your colleagues.

That rival who's killing it on social media...

...anything but yourself

Now's the time to go from excuses... to responsibility.

A phrase that I've always loved is that there is no wrong weather, just the wrong clothing. So, get your business jacket zipped up, and let's get on with it.

Don't *spend* your time, *invest* it.

Like a mechanic flipping the bonnet of a car and tuning up the engine, sometimes the smallest of adjustments can make a world of difference in the way you think about your time. Consider this observation:

Most people spend their time doing what they think they need to do, and then invest any leftover time they have in things like health, relationships, and personal development.

Others invest the time into making sure their health, relationships and personal development are in place, and then fit the things they think they need to do into the rest of their time.

You might say, well that's all very nice, but if I don't put the time into my work, I won't have the money to sustain my lifestyle.

That's a fair point, but it's also worth remembering that health, relationships and personal development are probably the things that you would describe as the most important things in your life. You see it all the time...

- The 'successful' businessperson who doesn't have time or energy to eat lunch or exercise.
- The kid who gets all the material things they want for Christmas, but deep down would swap them all for mum and dad to be home before they go to bed.
- The social media star who longs for a partner or family to share their life with.

You can't just stop working and spend all of your time at home doing nothing, I get that, but I bet you can improve the balance between those two parts of your life. More important than the process of allocating a certain number of hours to different areas of your life, are the outcomes you achieve from doing so. I call this PROPER balance, and I'll tell you more about that later.

For now, a good way to look at it is that it isn't about the time you put into things, but what you put into the *time*.

Invest 5%

In financial planning, it's common to invest a percentage of your income into something like a pension. In doing this, your money can multiply quickly.

The idea is that regular small amounts that you wouldn't miss in the short term can build up over the long term thanks to compound interest.

You should think of your personal development in the same way. Imagine if you invested just 5% of your working week into personal development. For most people that is only a couple of hours or maybe 20-30 minutes per working day. You can easily double up that time with something else by listening to audiobooks and podcasts whilst exercising/ commuting/ doing jobs around the house. That way you only need to be a bit more resourceful with the time you have instead of trying to free up more time in addition.

The value of personal development snowballs exponentially in the same way as a financial investment, because every day you can use all of the knowledge you've accumulated from the preceding days.

Start to invest 5% today. Your future self will thank you for it.

Value your time

What is the value of your time? Let's work it out.

- How much do you want to earn next year? (eg £50,000).
- Divide it by the number of weeks you want to work, taking into account holidays (eg £50,000 / 40 = £1,250).
- Divide that number by the number of hours you want to work per week (eg £1,250 / 30 = £41.66).
- Double that number to account for the non-billable tasks you will need to do during the week (eg £41.66 x2 = £83.33).

Very roughly speaking, that is your hourly value, and you can use it as a rough guide to decide how long to spend on certain things. For example, if a task is worth around £40 to you, you know you should try not to spend more than half an hour on it. If another task comes in that is worth £160 you can probably afford to spend a couple of hours on it. On the flipside of this, if it costs say £20 to outsource a task that would take you two hours to complete yourself... well, it all starts to make sense, doesn't it?

This is just a guide that you might find useful for time allocation, but it doesn't account for hours outside of the working hours you used in the calculation. Those hours are family time, health time and 'you' time. They are the most valuable hours you have, so don't under-sell them.

You may find it useful to view time as money, health and moments.

Profit is sanity

"Oh, he has an amazing business. He's made seven figures."

Have you ever heard something like this about someone, and then wondered why that same person seems to be struggling to pay their bills or is always touting for more work?

It's pretty common, and it comes from the misconception of what 'success' really is, and how the notion of 'figures' really translates.

On face value, we assume that if there are two businesses, and one turns over £75k whilst the other turns over £750k, the second one is the more successful. Not necessarily the case, especially if the first one has far lower operating costs or overheads, makes a higher profit, and therefore has more cash in the bank. I know countless small businesses that easily outperform bigger businesses in this way.

A well-known business phrase explains it best: 'Turnover is vanity. Profit is sanity'. I must look up who originally said that.

A big part of time mastery is productivity, and that comes from the efficiency of a person or business to achieve its purpose using minimal energy and time. Here are 6 simple ways that you can increase the profit margins in your business.

1. **Put your prices up.** If you demonstrate the value your product or service provides using real life testimonials, you can raise your prices to reflect the value of the outcome instead of the cost of your process.

When people view the price as a small percentage of the value they'll get from the results of working with you, it's far better than them thinking of it as a cost of hiring you for an agreed amount of time.

2. **Upsell to existing clients.** It's usually far more efficient to get more from your current clients than it is to onboard new ones. In already knowing them, you'll know what they'd benefit from; whether it's a separate thing or an extension of something you're currently providing for them that is already getting good results.

3. **Reduce your costs.** You might think this means totally cutting some things out, but you don't necessarily have to do that. You can normally streamline processes instead if you take the time to regularly review them and see just how much time or money you really need to spend on them.

4. **Ask more questions.** Most service providers will be happy for the opportunity to review your costs and try to give you a better deal than you currently get. You can usually get little extras if you ask, too, like free shipping and additional discounts for buying in bulk. As usual though, if you don't ask, you probably won't get.

5. **Automate.** Use tech to automate your business where you can. Many parts of things like admin, marketing, sales, accounting, customer service and workflow can all be automated through various bits of software and applications to save you a lot of time, which can instead be spent on profit generating activities.

6. **Create a passive income.** I'm not talking about taking on MLM stuff, here. I'm talking about adding a string to your existing bow from within your existing work/business. For example, if you often give advice or training on one particular area, maybe you can record a version of it and sell the video to other clients further down the line. This is just one example of many passive streams that are becoming more and more commonplace in business.

Whatever your goals, it's important to focus on the right things. Time may not be money, but making more profit on the business you conduct will get you to your targets more quickly – and therefore help you free up more time!

'Me' doesn't mean 'free'

Have you ever tried to justify how cost-saving a job was for you by having done the donkey work yourself? For example, re-decorating your front room or building your own website.

Please don't fall into the trap of thinking that the saving of money is more important than the saving of *time*. Let's face it, it may have saved you thousands fitting your new kitchen yourself, but when you take into account the hours you spent researching, learning, trying, failing, crying and trying again – and getting an average at best 'finish' in the outcome - might it have been less expensive overall to pay someone else to do it (properly) for you? Always consider how much it would cost you to hire 'you' to do that job when you're working out how profitable or cost-saving a job really is. You might be surprised.

This is not to say that you shouldn't do work yourself. It is simply a reminder to truly value your own time.

Don't say don't

Don't think of a pink elephant standing on a ball.

Don't.

You *did*, didn't you?

When teaching children earlier in my career, I learned to always say what I *did* want them to do rather than what I didn't want them to do.

"Walk through school", is way more effective than "Don't run".

"Listen carefully", is far better than "Don't interrupt".

"Do this", always gets a better response than "Don't do that".

We hear 'don't, and disregard it, focusing only on what comes next. That's why you pictured the pink elephant standing on the ball.

This isn't just for kids. Maybe you tell yourself:

- "Don't get distracted"
- "Don't keep your phone right next to you"
- "Don't take too much on and get overwhelmed"

This only serves to put in your mind the very thing that you don't want. It would be more effective if you changed that language to:

- "Stay focused"
- "Turn your phone off"
- "Carefully monitor your workload"

Your language is so important in determining the way you see the world. You may or may not believe in the law of attraction and the adage that you 'attract how you act', but one thing is for sure, you saw that pink elephant, didn't you?

Autopilot and flow

Have you ever started work in the morning, replied to a few emails, answered a few calls and then glanced up at the clock to find the whole day has passed and yet you can't put your finger on exactly what it is you've really achieved?

I would put good money on the fact that you've experienced something similar whilst in the car; completing an entire journey without any recollection of what happened on during the entire drive. I think we've all done that. Autopilot.

Isn't it scary to think you've been in the car for over an hour and travelled 40 miles at a high (but legal) speed, making decisions throughout the entire journey that you can't remember anything about. It happens all the time. You go into autopilot regularly. In fact, around half of what we do on a day-to-day basis is habitual, which probably explains why a day can seem to disappear so quickly.

Sometimes autopilot works with triggers for you to react to, and with things like notifications, colleagues, and customers, you probably have loads of them in a short space of time. This can add up to feel like a wasted day.

Your most productive days are those where you can achieve a state of 'flow'. You get stuck into a task and lose yourself in it. Your peripheral senses seem to switch off, and nothing around you can take your focus from what you are working on. It's in this state that you do your best work, so the ability to get into a flow state is invaluable.

The artist, Paul Klee, described the state he gets into when he paints in the zone. He said, "Everything vanishes around me, and works are born as if out of the void. Ripe, graphic fruits fall off. My hand has become the obedient instrument of a remote will". How many fruits will fall off for you today?

That was supposed to sound better than it did!

Let's move from art to sport. How amazing it is to see an athlete in a state of flow? Basketball fans will remember 'the shot' by Michael Jordan that overturned a losing scoreline with only 3 seconds remaining, to win the 1989 NBA Championship for the Chicago Bulls.

In a similar way, David Beckham took England to the 2002 football World Cup when he scored an added time free kick against Greece. "Nothing was going to stop me taking that free-kick. I felt confident, calm, certain. I knew I could make it", he said after the event.

In both sporting cases it was the defining moment that people remember, but on reflection, it is clear that both players were in a state of flow for an extended period of time. Jordan scored an impressive 44 points in that game for the Bulls, and Beckham's all-round performance throughout the World Cup Qualifying match was impressive to watch.

They were both 'in the zone'.

Both autopilot and flow can see the hours disappear very quickly, but the latter is a lot more productive than the former. It's time you learned to take more control of how much time you are willing to give, and how you are willing to give it.

Spend a good hour on it

What is an hour? 60 minutes? Two lots of 30 minutes? Four lots of 15 minutes?

Mathematically, all of the above answers are correct, but in terms of value it isn't always so simple, because it can take time to get into 'the zone' – that state of flow where you are fully concentrating on the task in hand and making great progress.

Let's assume it takes you 10 minutes to get there per task. If you were to split your hour in two parts (so two tasks), you'd spend 20 minutes in total getting into the zone. For 15-minute blocks you'd be spending more time *getting* there than *being* there.

Maybe it takes you less than 10 minutes to get into the zone, but it makes no difference to the principle, and this is why a work sprint of a solid hour could work a lot better than four separate sets of 15 minutes.

The length of time that you can stay productive in the zone varies from person to person, but with practice, you can improve the length of time you can stay focused for. I find that an hour is a nice balance of being a challenge but not being unattainable.

You do, of course need to stay undistracted throughout, and this is often the downfall for people.

It's predicted that office workers are distracted every 11 minutes, and each distraction can take up to 25 minutes to recover back to the same level of concentration from. Just run that maths through your mind and it's easy to see why distractions are one of the biggest time management challenges around.

You might never fully eliminate distractions, but you can certainly reduce them by:

- Working in a quiet place where possible. Off-site, where people are unlikely to bump into you or request your attention is perfect.
- Listening to music that helps you to focus (nothing you'll sing along to, though. Classical music is my favourite, even though I don't ordinarily listen to it at other times).
- Putting your headphones in. Yes, even if you have no music on, headphones can act as an extra deterrent to people who might just ask you for the time or whatever!
- Giving yourself permission to go DND (do not disturb). Switch calls and messages off and close your emails. You'd do it if you were in a meeting (I hope), so why not book a meeting with yourself? Tell colleagues you're unavailable for the next hour - and go.

Hopefully, some of the above can help you create the right environment to be productive. You can 'sprint' through a lot of quality work in an uninterrupted hour - just try it!

Remember, an hour is not simply the sum of its fragmented parts, because task shifting takes time. Spend a good hour on it. You'll see.

Expanding tasks

When my wife and I moved into our new house, I was looking forward to having more space (an extra bedroom and a slighter bigger kitchen). What I didn't account for was that we would take everything from the old house with us *and* add lots of new things as well. Turns out we didn't have more space after all.

Not to worry, I thought - we've got a loft in this new house. We can put the things that we want to keep (but don't really use) up there. I bet some of you smirked when you read that, didn't you? As you can imagine, it didn't take long before the loft was filled with loads of stuff that wasn't serving much of a purpose, but somehow, there still wasn't enough space in the liveable parts of the house. Where was everything going to fit?

"Darling, let's get a shed!" I'm sure you can guess how that suggestion to my wife panned out, but needless to say, there are lessons, here:

- The space in the house is just like the time you have in your working day. Everyone always wants more of it, but as soon as it's available, it gets filled up very quickly.

- The loft is like the overtime you put in by working late, checking emails in the evening, and catching up on a bit of paperwork at the weekend. It's handy at first but before long you're actively relying on that time.

- Getting the shed wasn't a good idea (my wife was right). It simply moved and multiplied the problem (our stuff) rather than solve it.

> **Working harder is only ever a short-term solution.**
> **Working smarter is the key to success.**

Some students sit on a 3-month university assignment deadline until the day before the due date, and then pull an all-nighter, working like mad to get it done. Similarly, you've probably experienced the 'last day before holiday' productivity rush, in which you manage to achieve more in the 6 hours before you're forced onto an aeroplane than you ordinarily would in 6 days.

Both scenarios are examples of Parkinson's Law, and if you aren't familiar with it yet, you really need to know about it. It applies to your house, your schedule, and pretty much every area of your life. It is the adage that things will always fill the space (large or small) that they are allocated.

So, when you have a deadline like the story of the student with the assignment, work smarter and break it into manageable sections with milestones. This approach allows you to complete the task in a series of small, manageable sprints, which is usually a lot less overwhelming than one big task, and will usually lead to a better quality final result, too.

> **Give yourself enough time to do the job well - but no longer.**
> **If you have too long to do something,**
> **you'll take too long to do it.**

The gold medal grafter

All serious athletes - regardless of discipline - have to adopt a lifestyle that keeps them at their physical and mental peak. That lifestyle often represents sacrifice, especially to people who love the idea of winning itself but don't love the idea of preparing to win. They can imagine themselves holding aloft the trophy, but won't push themselves in the gym or go out for a run on a cold, wet morning. They can imagine the million-dollar contracts and sponsorships, but can't say no to the offer of a burger and a beer.

When Muhammad Ali said, "The fight is won or lost far away from witnesses – behind the lines, in the gym, and out there on the road, long before I dance under those lights", he highlighted the importance of working **on** his performance so that he could excel **in** his performance on fight night.

When it comes to your business, it is often said that you should make time to work **on** your business as well as **in** it, but do you actually do it?

You probably know that you'll never be a successful athlete if you don't train hard and maintain a disciplined lifestyle (and it's not guaranteed even if you *do*, to be fair), so why should achieving success in business be any different?

When you make time to work **on** your business you can experience many benefits including:

- Management of your energy levels by planning what to eat and drink
- Automation of parts of your business to save you time and stress
- Development of processes in your business to help you to stay consistent as you scale
- A better understanding of each aspect of the customer journey within your business, so that you can make regular, incremental improvements to it.

Train hard and then recover

Along with a willingness to work hard, athletes clearly understand the need for sufficient rest and recovery. They know that training hard for 12 hours straight on a regular basis will do more harm than good in the long run. They don't want to injure themselves, so they make time to get enough sleep and 'down time'.

Business people commonly make the mistake of working late into the night and then starting early the next day on a regular basis. OK, so you may not pull a hamstring, but it will certainly have an adverse effect on your physical and mental performance at work if you aren't giving yourself time to recover properly.

Fail to prepare, prepare to fail

When the athlete's schedule is planned, it is carefully crafted to have plenty of recovery time in between bouts of intense activity, that stretch the athlete's capabilities without overwhelming them. The perfect balance is a session that takes the athlete just outside their comfort zone; further than they have been before, but within reach to that point where they get completely into 'the zone' with a mindset of, "Come on. You can do this!"

If most business people I know were athletes and tried to continue with their current mentality, they'd not bother with the recovery and instead likely schedule a 100-mile sprint with ankle weights before lunch. That may seem ridiculous, and it is, but it is incredible how much people try to cram into their day on a regular basis; setting themselves up for failure, stress and probably an early grave.

Do yourself a favour and schedule time to schedule your time. You'll read this piece of advice regularly throughout this book because, frankly, it is very important, and I want it to sink into your mind. It is such an important thing to do as it has a knock-on effect to tons of other things. In this case, it will give you the time to carefully plan your day to take you to that perfect level and put you in the zone.

"Come on. You can do this!"

Build strength and condition yourself for success

Remember, athletes build strength through placing stress on their muscle fibres and creating micro-tears that repair stronger. If they overdo it, they get injured, it's as simple as that. They work to a realistic plan to achieve their goals. In the case of Olympic athletes, this usually starts with a 4-year periodic training plan. Yes, it's really that long.

In general, people overestimate what they can achieve in a day and underestimate what they can achieve in a year.

Follow the same principle in your business life. Stretch yourself to achieve great things, but don't overdo it - or you'll do more damage than you realise.

Fuel yourself with the right things

Most Strength and Conditioning coaches would agree that an athlete's diet is even more of a contributing factor to their overall physical condition than any training programme. Top athletes are very deliberate about the things they put into their body and they reap the benefits of it in their energy levels (amongst other things).

Business people, due to being 'busy', often start the day without breakfast, grab lunch on the go if they remember, and top their energy levels up all day with coffee and snacks. The effects this has to your energy levels is huge, so making the time to work **on** fuelling yourself with the right food and drink so that you can benefit from more energy **in** your day is a smart move.

Get in the right frame of mind

Before every training session and performance, top athletes take time to warm up mentally and physically. Not only does this get them physically ready but it also puts them into the right frame of mind for what is to follow.

Why don't business people do this?

Your workday warm up could include:

- A short walk to wake you up, get your heart pumping and get fresh air into your lungs.
- A bowl of cereal or a few slices of toast to give you some slow-release carbohydrates for energy throughout the morning.
- A glass of water. It is believed that 1% dehydration can impact performance by 10%. When you first wake up in the morning you have more than likely just had several hours without a drink – and you'll have lost sweat, too.
- Mentally preparing for the day by checking your schedule and visualising how you want some key parts of your day to go.

The psychology–physiology link is really interesting and under-utilised. Basically, we all accept that feeling sad and self-conscious will show in our body language, as would a feeling of confidence and happiness. You may have heard of 'power poses' and things like that, but if you're like most people you're probably thinking, 'I'm not doing that in the office, I'll look a right idiot'. You're probably right, but there is in fact some pretty strong evidence to show that it would in fact make you feel more confident to do it. You see, it works the other way, too. If being happy makes you laugh, laughing can make you happy. If public speaking makes you nervous and your breathing speed up, consciously slowing it down with some breathing exercises can help you to feel calmer about presenting.

There is a lot to be said for the subtle little things you can do to help yourself perform at your best.

The pre-match huddle

Before team games, team mates often have a 'huddle' right before the first whistle. This helps them to clarify what they expect from each other and sharpen their focus. There's a bonding element, too, of course.

Huddles can work well at work, too. It doesn't have to be a formal meeting, just a quick reminder of what you are striving for and a little bit of a nudge to get everyone going in the right direction.

Half time

The next thing athletes often benefit from is half time. During this short time, they will usually rest and replenish their energy levels with a carefully selected snack and drink, whilst reflecting on how the first half has gone and making any necessary adjustments to the game plan before getting themselves motivated for a big second half.

At work, would a half time be useful for you? I expect it would. Regardless of how the morning has gone, you should take a short break to boost your energy levels and refocus your mind for the 'second half'.

Cool down

After the game or event, athletes go through a cool down. They do this for a few reasons, and a lot of these can be applied to a business setting:

- *They slowly bring their heart rate back down to prepare themselves for a lower intensity of activity.*
  Taking some time to review your day and tie up any loose ends would help you to prepare for a relaxing evening at home with your family.
- *They talk about the performance, what went well, and what needs some work in upcoming training sessions.*
  If you spent a few minutes thinking about what you need to work on in the coming week as a result of today's performance, you

could get it programmed into your schedule so that you can relax in the knowledge it is in hand rather than have it buzzing around your head.

Going for gold

I speak to lots of business people who you could say are going for gold in their business and their life. They tell me they have been so busy in their business and they 'need to find time' to work on it. Sometimes, it's so that they can make more money, and sometimes, it's to allow them to take better care of themselves and their relationships. Either way, you will never 'find' time to become the best you can be – you have to *make* time.

Level Two

Block 6

Productivity

Understand Parkinson's Law

When I first started my business, I was keen to make a success of it, so naturally I put a lot of time into it - usually six days per week at least. Why? Because that's what you need to do when you run your own business, isn't it? Well, that's what I thought until one of the worst times of my life persuaded me otherwise.

Around 10 years ago, my Mum had mysteriously fallen down the stairs twice in the space of a few weeks. Both times she couldn't recall how it had happened, but with bumps, bruises and a broken hip to show for it, she certainly caused herself a lot of damage. It took a long while for doctors to pinpoint the cause, but she was finally diagnosed with Progressive Supranuclear Palsy: a degenerative, terminal brain disease with no treatment and no cure. She was given the (frighteningly accurate) prediction that she would live for around another 6 years, but that during those years she would steadily lose her ability to balance, walk, eat, drink, see, and communicate.

That kind of news hits you like a train. Goodness knows how hard it must have been for Mum to hear those words said about herself. I say goodness knows, because not once did I ever hear her complain. I really don't know how that's possible.

It suddenly became so clear to me how finite and precious time really is, and whilst feeling powerless to make things better, I knew what I needed to do. I immediately cut down my working week to spend a full day every Friday with Mum, have some good times together, and really get to know her properly.

I was willing to accept whatever impact that had on my business, but work didn't feel like the best use of my time anymore, to be honest. Surprisingly, however, I was amazed at how easy it was to get everything done in less time. I just became a lot stricter with how I invested the time I had, cut unnecessary things out of the picture, and streamlined/outsourced processes wherever possible. I wasn't just protecting my time anymore, I was protecting my 'Mum-time', and I wasn't going to give that up without a fight. As it happens, I spent every Friday with Mum for those 6 years, and the business didn't suffer at all. That was a lesson to me in itself.

I'll never forget receiving the phone call from my brother on Christmas morning 2015, to tell me that Mum had passed away. Nothing prepares you for that, even when it isn't completely unexpected. I had always been really close to Mum, and I'll always look back with fondness on those Fridays we spent together, in which I probably got to know her better than I would've done if none of this had ever happened. She was a remarkable lady who deserved more time.

Parkinson's Law in your business

Get into good habits by blocking out time every week specifically for reflecting on how you are doing things.

You may find it useful to consider these questions:

1. **What are the key drivers of your success?** The things that, without question, need to happen for the business to succeed. Just like a VIP list at a night club, if it isn't on the list, it's not coming in.

2. **Of those things on the list, which are essential for you to do personally?** There are normally things that you could outsource or delegate to free up some of your time without any adverse effect on the business. Find them.

3. **If you could free up a day, how would you use it?** If the goal is powerful enough, you'll find the motivation to make the positive changes you need in order to free up that time.

Understand Parkinson's Law

Perfection paralysis

You can probably relate to this.

You spend ages working on something, and just as you are getting to the end of it, you start to question whether the whole thing was worth it.

You worry how it will be received - and start to imagine all the ways that it isn't good enough.

In the end, you delete it, so all that time you spent working on it was wasted. It was actually pretty good, too.

Doing doesn't pay the bills. *Done* does.

Time hacks to free up time quickly

When you are overwhelmed and need to free up some time quickly, consider these suggestions:

Decide what NOT to do. The Pareto principle says that 80% of your results come from only 20% of the things you do. List everything you need to do on a list numbered by priority. Start with the one that takes you closest to your goal.

It would be naïve to think that you can just discard the 80% of tasks that are not in your priority 20%, but I guarantee there will be things in there that you can either *not* do completely - or spend less time doing.

Get some tasks off your plate. Using your list, label each item as A, B or C.

- **A = Must be done by you.** You're the only one who can do it and there's no way of teaching anyone else to do it.

- **B = Could be taught.** You are the only one who can do it, but you could teach someone else to do it. A common excuse it 'it'd take me longer to show someone else to do it than it would to just do it myself'. If it's a one-off task, this may be a fair argument, but if it's a task that will come up again (and again), it is worth the investment of time on this occasion if it means you won't have to do it yourself ever again. Even better than teaching one person to do it is if you can record the process so that others can learn from it in future.

- **C = Needs to be done, but not necessarily by you.** Examples are things like answering calls, graphic design and writing copy. Outsource (or delegate) them. It'll save you hours, doesn't have to cost the Earth, and if you get the right person to do it then the results will probably be better than if you did it yourself anyway.

Do the As, start to delegate the Bs, and definitely outsource the Cs.

If you can, charge up front. You won't waste time chasing invoices, worrying about being paid, or doing any work that there's a chance you won't be paid for.

Double up on tasks (but don't multi-task). There is a big difference between doubling up and multi-tasking. Multi-tasking is trying to do two things at the same time that both require you to think about them (bad idea), like doing a VAT return and a sales email at the same time, or typing a text message whilst driving (please – never do that). Doubling up is doing something that doesn't need your conscious attention at the same time as something that does. For example, making a call whilst out walking the dog, or listening to an audiobook whilst travelling to work on the train. Doubling up like this can save you the time it takes to do tasks that don't need much conscious attention.

Let it go to voicemail. People often ask questions that they could pretty easily find out the answers to themselves. Have a select few people that you will always answer calls from, but with anyone else, let it go to voicemail. Unless it's urgent (genuinely), give them a call back in an hour or two. A lot of the time you will find that they'll tell you they managed to sort it. Try it, it works.

Work in shifts. If you work with other people, set shifts for answering calls. That way you can have a solid hour where you know you will be able to get stuck into what you need to be doing without distraction. There may be the odd occasion where an emergency means you need to be distracted right away, but most of the time people will accept that you are 'on another call' or 'in a meeting' and be happy for you to return their call within a reasonable time period.

Take control of your notifications. Lots of people will tell you they get distracted by social media, messages and emails in their working day, yet they spend it sitting in front of a screen with their phone right next to them on the desk. Whenever they get an email or social media update, their phone lights up and a big box appears on their computer screen. Both are often accompanied by an alert sound of some sort. Is it any wonder it distracts them? Whether you switch your notifications off entirely or just manage the settings on each one is up to you, but either way you should be selective and deliberate about how you set things up.

Set an email auto reply. You may be worried about missing an important email (most people say that's why they check them so much), but an auto reply can set the expectation of when the sender can expect a response from you. It may be within a couple of hours, or even at the end of the day. Whatever it is, you need to set the rules of the game if you want people to follow them. In the case of emergencies, you can suggest that they call, but ideally this should be a number that is monitored by someone other than you! As an example, you may write something like 'Thank you for your email. In the interests of being as productive as possible I only check my emails every few hours, so I will get back to you at my earliest opportunity. If you need me urgently, please call the office on (number)'.

Don't reply to non-urgent messages straight away. In my experience this can create a monster. If you reply immediately it can set an expectation that you will indeed always reply immediately. Without this expectation, people are typically happy to wait a reasonable time for a response. Think about it; how long do you think is an acceptable time to wait for a reply to an email / voicemail / social media message / text? As a rule of thumb, I would personally have no problem with waiting 24 hours for an email response, and a few hours for a call back or text reply. It's completely fair to expect that someone is with another client or working on another project for an entire day.

Switch off smart phone notifications. I know we've already touched on this, but it's a big one. Bleeps, flashes, buzzes... app notifications can be a nightmare. Silence them. Your phone should be serving you on your terms – not the other way around.

Book a 'meeting'. We're more disciplined in meetings, so book a meeting with yourself in the calendar. Take yourself offline and off site to get stuck into some work you need to do.

Limit tasks. Select your tasks based on the amount of time their potential outcomes deserve. Too often, we book an hour for things by default, but Parkinson's Law tells us that things will expand to the space that they are given, so if it deserves 10 minutes, make it 10 minutes. If it isn't clear what the outcomes will be, don't do it at all.

Downgrade and delete. Some face-to-face meetings could be online. Some online meetings could be an email. Some emails could be a quick call. Some quick calls could be a text. Some texts aren't needed at all! Use the method that takes the least time, without taking away from the message itself.

Feel the fear and ask it anyway. Do you know the number one reason why people don't get what they want? That's right, it's because they don't ask for it. If you need some help with something, ask. If you need a short extension on a deadline, ask. If you want to work with someone, ask. It's important to remember that if you don't ask you don't get, so even if you do ask and you still don't get, you aren't in any worse position than you would've been. The law of averages says that if you ask enough reasonable questions, some will get a successful response and free up valuable time for you. Ask more questions... it's a numbers game.

Get clear on the non-negotiables. When you are planning for today it is pretty easy to visualise what needs to be done, but looking to next week, next month and next year can be more difficult. The further into the future you try to see, the more blurred the picture becomes because there are so many possibilities and things that may arise. The way around this is to consider your non-negotiables. For example, apart from some scheduled catch ups or reviews that are booked in advance, you probably won't know everything you'll have to do in 3 weeks' time. You can, however plan in the things that you definitely want to commit to regardless of what else comes up, like time with family and time for your health. Successful people know they're going to be busy and that they'll never 'find' time to go to the gym, never mind have a week off. They know that they need to plan ahead, so they block out certain times in their calendar at the start of the year. These things are the non-negotiables and it goes without saying that not doing them isn't an option, so you need to book them in.

Listen to audio a little bit quicker. If you're listening to an audiobook for enjoyment, you may not want to do this, but if you're purely listening to it to take in the information it has to offer, then you can set the recording to play more quickly. I have found that anything quicker than x1.5 is a bit too much for me, but x1.25 can save you an hour on a 5-hour audiobook and really doesn't sound much different.

Time hacks can help you to free up some time straight away. Everything in the list works for some people, but they probably won't all be right for you. If just one of them works for you, great! Once you've freed up a little bit of time, you'll want to make the most of it. *Time Habits* can help you to make the most of whatever time you have.

Freeing up more time only gives you more capacity for the things you do already, so if you are a procrastinator with more time you'll probably just procrastinate for longer. If your meetings overrun and you have more time, your meetings will last even longer. And if you are guilty of trying to cram too much into a day, you'll still do that with more time. It's a matter of resource and resourcefulness.

Time habits permanently change the things you do routinely and improves your resourcefulness so that you can make the most of your time, however much of it you have.

This is an essential part of your life because around half of the things you do every day are habitual. In the absence of a conscious decision to not do something, you will automatically do the thing that you habitually do in a given situation.

An example of this is dieting. People can make good progress towards achieving their weight loss goals by following a diet and by consciously avoiding certain foods that they would normally eat a lot of. The problem comes when they get to their goal weight and slip back into old habits, going back to how they were before.

It's a similar story with personal development books and seminars. You often finish or leave them feeling pumped up, but then gradually you go back to how you were feeling previously.

Habits are repeat behaviours, and they need to be replaced. That's why the hacks need the habits.

How to be brilliant with tech

Technology is the single biggest reason why you should be able to achieve way more every day than has ever been possible before. Unfortunately, it is also the number one reason why you *don't*.

Tech can be both a blessing and a curse.

By making it work for you rather than against you, you will be achieving a double win. You'll be creating a great ally whilst simultaneously defeating a formidable opponent. It is undoubtedly a key battle for you to win as you strive for time mastery.

Every day, technology is advancing, so there is a very strong chance that any specific advice written here would be outdated fairly quickly. For that reason, each of the following points is coupled with a general principle that I believe will be relevant even when the specific details cease to be.

Calendar automation. How often have you had a long, time-consuming, back-and-forth conversation with someone that goes like this:

"How about Tuesday 9am?"

- *I can't do Tuesdays, sorry. How about Wednesday?*

"What time?"

- *11.30 or 1pm.*

"Sorry I have something at 12pm so wouldn't be able to."

- *Thursday 3pm?*

"That might be ok. I'll have to get back to you tomorrow, though..."

People waste so much time booking suitable times to meet. Automating the process makes things easier, and there are various free apps available to help you to do that easily. You send the person a link to the spaces in your calendar, they book the one that suits them best from what's still available, and voila!

Just make sure the preferences are set as you want them, so that people can only book at times that you would be happy for them to do so.

Apps like Doodle are equally as good for finding the best time for a *group* of people to meet. Set up plenty of options, send the link to everyone and the app will report back to you with the most popular time that people can all do.

Drag and drop. If you use Outlook for your emails, you may or may not be aware that you can drag and drop emails into your calendar. This is great for things that you need to do, but you don't have time to do right now. You can allocate it an appropriate space in your schedule and relax in the knowledge that you won't forget it or miss it.

Text replacement. Depending on the devices you use, you may have a 'text replacement' feature (Apple products do, and others have similar). It basically allows you to create a shortcut to a particular phrase or paragraph that you write regularly. For example, you could set up a shortcut that types out your business address, postcode, office number and basic directions whenever you type 'b.ad' or similar. This is really useful if you send out similar messages repeatedly.

Good CRM. A good Customer Relationship Management system is a great investment for most businesses, and there are options for every budget (including free).

It's always a good idea to have all of your notes organised and know where you are up to with everything. CRM possibilities are endless. If you haven't got one, you should consider it. HubSpot are popular and have free options.

Processes. Lots of businesses have processes that are stuck in someone's head, which is a problem when you want to develop the business. By putting processes into a system instead, you can make induction and ongoing training far easier. There are lots of options, but as a starting point, something as simple as a shared folder of 'live' (everyone can edit them) documents can be a good way of sharing and developing processes as the business grows. Add a little bit to them regularly and before long you'll have a pretty good guide for everyone in your business.

Automation. There are so many things you can automate, from invoicing, receipt input and bank reconciliation, to email responses, repeat calendar entries and sales. The beauty of automation is that you don't need to remember to do things – as long as you've set it up properly it will just be done for you! As with most things, there are a lot of options depending on budget and what exactly the tasks are they you're automating. Start with one thing and build from there!

Simplicity. When you have multiple tabs open on your screen, it slows your computer down and it slows you down, too. I have seen people trying to work with emails, social media and instant messages popping up all over the screen. There's no way you can be productive with that going on, I don't care what you say!

Having lots of distractions is terrible for your ability to focus. Be as simplistic as you can with your tech.

Digitise everything you can. It's easy to lose papers. I think everyone would agree with that. Having things digitally allows you to access them wherever you are, securely, and at your convenience. How many photos have you got that you never look at? I really enjoy the face recognition feature on Google Photos. It allows me to see pictures of certain people much more easily, and of course the date and map facilities make it easy to find any photos from a particular time or place.

Down time. Mobile devices blur lines between work and leisure time, which can have a negative impact on mental health. We have spoken about PROPER balance, and technology needs to fall in line with that.

Smart phones really are smart. Unfortunately, the same can't always be said for their users! I saw a stat that the average person in the UK checks their smartphone 28 times per day. This is the inevitable cloud that is attached to the silver lining of benefits. Smart phones are designed to keep you engaged for as long as possible. Kind of like that person you know you could call to answer your question but would keep you on the phone for an hour and you wouldn't be able to escape.

You've got to make some rules about when you'll detach yourself from tech and just be human.

You can set the notifications to only ring for certain people, so you can avoid distractions from every man and his dog without worrying about missing an emergency call from whoever you set as your VIP numbers.

Simply putting the phone out of reach helps, whether at home or work. You can still hear it if it rings, but having to stand up to go and get it takes away the temptation to flick the phone up every 30 seconds as a habit of 'just checking'. Sometimes, you don't even realise you're doing it.

Shortcuts. Whatever programmes you use on a regular basis, whether Zoom, Office, Outlook or anything else, it's a good idea to take some time to learn some keyboard shortcuts that perform specific tasks. There are hundreds for most programmes and you can easily find them with a simple Google search. Don't try to learn them all at once. Just choose a couple to start with and build on it once you get used to them. They really do save you a lot of time and you may be pleasantly surprised!

When it comes to your productivity, tech is full of wins and losses. It saves you time and then steals it again. You win a battle, then you lose one. At the end of the day, it's OK to lose some battles as long as you make sure you win more than you lose overall. If you can achieve that every day, you're doing pretty well.

Level Two

Block 7

Organisation

Why Wile E Coyote could never catch the Road Runner

You are probably familiar with Wile E Coyote and his ongoing struggle in catching the Road Runner. He had tons of ideas in those fantastic Warner Brothers cartoons. In fact, he was actually very creative, but something was always missing from his master plans.

Like many others with big goals, the idea of a quick win was always highly attractive to Wile E. Short-of-time business owners will surely relate to that, because there's seemingly never enough time to do everything, is there? Catching that Road Runner as soon as possible was the only thing on our coyote's mind.

Some of the quick-win ideas he had, like attaching himself to a rocket, were of course crazy. But on reflection, the old canine actually had some half decent ideas. He once placed some food to entice the Road Runner into the perfect spot, directly beneath a trap that he would quickly and quietly lower down onto his prey when he least expected it from the cliff above. It seemed like a decent idea.

A common theme in Wile E's woes was a careless mistake or oversight of some kind. A careless oversight that a bit more thought and planning could easily have avoided. In the case of the trap, he got his foot tangled in the rope and found himself, once again, plummeting towards the ground, bracing himself for pain, and wondering where it had all gone wrong.

Road Runner ate the food, heard the struggle, and with a quick 'Beep Beep', he was gone for another day.

> **Busy business people and Wile E Coyote actually have quite a lot in common.**

It's just a cartoon, you may say, and you'd be right, but there are some comparisons that can be made to how many business owners utilise their time. Here are just a few:

1. **They have so many ideas** - That can be a good thing, but it can be hard to give enough focused attention to any of them if you're thinking about too many at once. Ideas are like rabbits; a couple can become a dozen very quickly, and if you try to keep them all, things soon get out of control. It's usually more important to look after the ones you have than to make more of them.

2. **They are determined and hungry to succeed** - They know exactly what they want and have their eyes firmly on the prize. Unfortunately, they can sometimes get tunnel vision and fail to see the warning signs that are all around them. It's usually better to step back and take a moment to assess the situation before jumping in at the deep end.

3. **They are excited to get going straight away** - Here's the problem. They are reactive to every opportunity, and often over-face themselves with things, which can unfortunately lead to careless, avoidable mistakes.

So, the old saying goes, 'Fail to Prepare, Prepare to Fail'. We all know it, but people do exactly this every day. Just like Wile E Coyote, they jump straight into their busy day and work hard, but working harder is only ever a short-term solution. The key to achieving more in less time lies with working smarter, not harder.

If Wile E Coyote had planned smarter and prepared a bit better, I'm sure he could've caught that Road Runner. I guess that would have ruined the cartoon, but it won't ruin your business. In fact, it'll make it a whole lot better.

Here's a tip to help get you into the habit of preparing more effectively and working smarter: Schedule time to schedule your time.

It doesn't have to take a long time to schedule your time. Just 10 minutes of looking over your schedule for the week ahead can enable you to 'ACME': **A**nticipate, **C**onfirm, **M**ove, **E**valuate. Turns out the answer was right in front of Wile E Coyote all along!

Anticipate any problems that might come up (eg driving through town at rush hour)

Confirm details to avoid wasted journeys (eg meeting details, desired outcomes)

Move meetings to make sense (eg blocking two meetings in the same/ similar location one after the other)

Evaluate whether the things in your schedule are all necessary

Here's how that can look in practice for Wile E Coyote (and for you, too):

ACME for Wile E

Anticipate: You often end up falling off cliffs. Avoid cliffs.

Also, if you are planning to ride a rocket from 0-100mph, plan a way to safely get from 100-0mph, too!

Confirm: Some of your plans have been ruined by something not being connected properly, like a rope or a cable. Have a practice run before the main event to make sure it works.

Move: A lot of your traps are out in the open. Consider luring the Road Runner to an enclosed space where speed is not as much of an advantage

Evaluate: Lots of your ideas are poor but you have some good ones. Get rid of the ones that include rockets, anvils and cliffs, and concentrate on things that almost worked, like using free bird feed.

ACME for you

Anticipate: You quite often find yourself in rush hour traffic. Try to schedule any off-site meetings between 11am and 2pm so you can miss that traffic completely. Alternatively, get the train or meet virtually (if appropriate) if all participants are comfortable doing so.

If you do end up with an unavoidable 4pm city centre meeting, take some admin tasks that you can do remotely and piece it all together so you can travel at the best time. Using cloud-based software where possible helps to automate this. Personally, I can access any of my work remotely at any time and it's so useful.

Confirm: Have you ever been to a meeting with someone who forgot to bring something they needed, or even worse they got the time wrong and didn't show up at all?

It's worth getting into the habit of always confirming meetings in advance. When you schedule a meeting, set an alert to remind you to send a "looking forward to our meeting at your office today at 3pm" message.

Move: Too many people think day-to-day, but it's much better to think week-to-week.

If you have two meetings in a similar area on different days, enquire whether it would be possible to move one to fit with your other - and therefore halve your travel. Most people are pretty accommodating if given enough notice.

Evaluate: Look at your upcoming week and write a clear outcome next to each scheduled item. If it's unclear or ambiguous, remove it - or at least control it (make it a call / virtual meeting and set a clear and appropriate timeframe for it). You could send a message like this: "Hi John. Thanks for your invite to meet. I want to answer your questions without taking up too much of your time, so how about we have a 10-minute call and then if we find we need to follow up afterwards we can do". If it's a task, give it a deadline. A task is only worth as much time as its outcome deserves, remember.

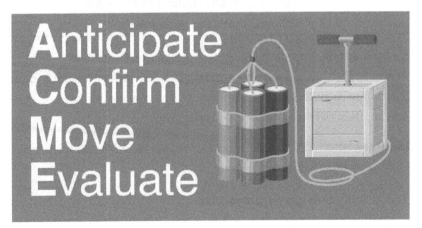

> **When you want to get organised,**
> **Then schedule time to schedule your time.**

How do I know which things to prioritise?

When it comes to prioritisation, Dwight D Eisenhower's famous 'Urgent and Important Quadrant' has undoubtedly been the go-to model for many decades. It is a model that encourages the categorisation of tasks by Importance and Urgency, to help decide when, whether and how to prioritise them.

I love the model and have used it many times. However, in many conversations with business owners over recent years, there is a recurring problem that arises with applying it. Whilst the principles ring true, it could be argued that in a world full of instant messages, social media and GPS tracking, life is different now than it used to be, and that creates challenges in task categorisation and prioritisation.

> **Everything is Urgent and Important these days.**
> **At least, that's the perception.**

An increasingly popular feeling amongst modern business owners is that they feel patronised and almost offended that you would think what they're doing is not important. If it wasn't important, they reason, then they wouldn't be doing it!

Here's an alternative model that focuses on activity and what tasks look like when they're being done.

The Activity Categorisation model

Following the same 'quadrant' structure as the Urgent and Important model, the Activity Categorisation model is made up of the following four sections:

(Re)active - Working in your business, eg: Doing things that keep the business going, such as delivering any technical work you have committed to, responding to day-to-day challenges, and communicating with customers, colleagues and stakeholders.

Allow time for this, but don't let it take your whole day.

Proactive - Working on your business, eg: Doing things that develop your business, such as strategy planning, sales, marketing, upskilling yourself/your team, and working on processes.

Schedule as much time for this as realistically possible.

Overactive - Busyness in your business, eg: Involving yourself in time-consuming things that need doing - but not necessarily by you - such as design work, copywriting, and admin.

Try to outsource this to a specialist.

Inactive - Not actively working, eg: Health and wellbeing time away from work to recover mentally and physically, time to think, time to enjoy, and time to build and maintain relationships.

Be intentional about this and don't underestimate its importance.

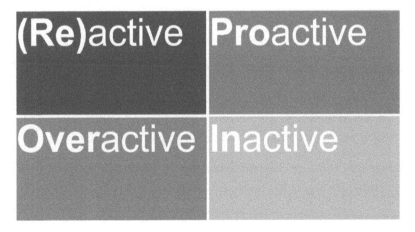

There are crossovers and inter-dependencies within this model, so it's important to get the balance right. For example:

- Proactively putting systems, plans and processes in place means you can reduce or eliminate the things you need to be reactive to. You should make as much time as you can to proactively improve your business.

- Equally, if you don't allow time to react to the day to day challenges your business faces, you'll probably fall behind and have to sacrifice some of your inactive time. Allocate enough time to do what you need to, but no more. Parkinson's Law has already taught you that if you allow more time than you need, you'll take it.

- If you spend too much time being overactive, you might not have time for anything else. Outsourcing tasks to specialists is often a very efficient move. They'll do it better than you can, in less time, and also free you up to do other things that will improve the business.

- Without recovery periods of inactivity, you might think you're being proactive, but you'll probably not be as productive or effective in doing anything. You need to allow yourself to recover if you want to operate at a high level. Not only that, but you'll also surprise yourself how creative your mind can be when it has the freedom to disconnect from the task in hand and search for the solutions to the challenges you may be facing. Trust me, taking a few moments to quietly enjoy solitude and stillness could well turn out to be the most productive activity of your day.

Give it a try. Capture everything you need to do on a list and categorise each one into one of the '**activity**' categories.

> **When reviewing your schedule,**
> **Then think of ACME.**

If doctors ran your business

I have spoken with many people over the years who struggle with the reactive side of their business. The calls, emails and constant change is certainly a challenge to deal with, and in many cases, it detracts from time that could be spent on proactive tasks that can improve processes and develop the business.

A good example of an organisation with a huge reactive responsibility is a hospital. They have a constant line of people to treat but also have to be ready for the possibility that they may have to drop everything to deal with an emergency situation as a priority.

If there's a heart attack they drop everything. But they don't walk out of an appointment with someone who's broken their leg for someone else who's broken both legs. It's a matter of priorities.

One thing for sure is that answering the phone, prescribing medication, and performing surgery doesn't all fall to the same person. If it did, they'd be rushed off their feet and probably go mad within a day on shift. I'd also love to know what their job title would be.

How does this apply to your business? Do you do everything yourself? Do 'urgent' situations take your focus away from some of the 'important but not urgent' things? There is probably quite a lot you can learn by thinking about how doctors would run your business.

It is believed that these days, customers expect that businesses will be open from 8am-8pm rather than 9am-5pm, and that expectation will only grow in the world of instant gratification that we live in.

Larger businesses with a staff rota might be ok with this, but for small businesses and freelancers it will be important to set boundaries and protect your time if the lion's share of the work falls to you.

As many people have said before, you should work to live, not the opposite.

The big rocks

A famous story about a professor demonstrates prioritisation really well. It starts with a glass jar, some rocks, pebbles and sand. The challenge is to fit everything into the jar, so the professor pours in the sand and then puts the pebbles in. The pebbles sit on top of the sand and don't leave enough space for the rocks.

The professor explains that the demonstration is a metaphor for time management. The jar represents the time you have. The grains of sand are the little things that come up and take up a lot of your time. The pebbles are important things you need to do at work, and the big rocks are the most important things in your life, such as health and relationships.

Once establishing that it is impossible to fit everything into the jar in this way, the professor empties the jar and starts again. This time, he puts the big rocks into the jar first, followed by the pebbles. He then pours the sand on top and it falls easily into all the gaps and spaces between the rocks and pebbles. Everything fits into the jar using this method.

By scheduling the big rocks into your life first, you are prioritising your health and relationships. Deep down you know that this is the most important thing, and it will have a positive impact on everything else you do.

Next you should schedule the important work tasks you need to do, giving each one the time it deserves and needs. No less and no more. After all, you wouldn't waste £50 on something that was barely worth a fiver, would you? Treat your time with the same respect.

Only then should you allow other, much smaller things into your schedule. Here is an example of this in action:

Schedule the big rocks first.

07.30-07.45	Have breakfast
07.45-08.15	Go for a walk with the dog
08.15-08.30	Call your friend
12.30-13.00	Have lunch
18.30	Enjoy an evening meal with your family

Then schedule the pebbles second.

07.30-07.45	Have breakfast
07.45-08.15	Go for a walk with the dog

08.15-08.30	Call your friend

08.45-09.30	*Send out invoices*
09.30-10.00	*Make final preparations for the team meeting*

12.30-13.00	Have lunch
13.00-13.30	*Important team meeting*
13.30-13.45	*Schedule follow up activities from the meeting*

14.00-14.30	*Make 5 sales calls*

15.00-17.00	*Client work*

17.30	Finish work for the day
18.30	Enjoy an evening meal with your family

Wiggle room – the sand

The 'rocks and pebbles' in this example have been scheduled with gaps in between. This gives wiggle room to prevent one overrunning task from impacting on all of the others. This then opens up time to deal with some 'sand'.

One example of sand in this metaphor is when someone asks if you're 'free for a chat today'. When you've got a block of time available (as in the example) it might be tempting to say "I'm free from 10.00-12.30, call whenever in that timeframe", but there are dangers in doing this:

- If they select 10.00, they can and will take up a huge chunk of your time because they know you're free

- If they select 12.15, then there's every risk they will over-run and take this away from your lunch break

- They call just as you're getting into the flow of another task in that down time.

In these circumstances, I like to think that 'specific is terrific'. So, it's much better to give an exact timeframe for things when people ask for that chat. You could say 'I've got 10 minutes at 10.00', which would leave you with a good chunk of your time available and also set the expectation of how long you can chat for.

Multiple entry tasks

Some tasks can require multiple calendar entries. For example, a meeting could have the following entries:

- Prepare and send out the meeting agenda
- Meeting preparation
- The meeting
- Complete actions arising from the meeting

It can be stressful to constantly have the Xs and Ys associated with Z buzzing around in your subconscious mind.

If you don't diarise each part of the overall task you run the risk of leaving loose ends and forgetting to do important things relating to the meeting - the kind of things that wake you up at 3am one morning and torment you!

There are many different tasks that require multiple entries. Scheduling time to schedule your time gives you a regular opportunity to consider this and ensure that you always do the things that you need to do.

Double up

Where possible, doubling up on tasks can help. As explained in the Time hacks section of this book, this is very different to multi-tasking and is advisable providing only one task requires your active attention. In the example given in this section, calling your friend and going for a walk can share the same time slot quite happily (watch out for traffic, obviously). There are plenty of other things you can double up on, but make sure you are clear about the boundary line between doubling up and multi-tasking!

Make your business your best client

A common mistake is to neglect your own business in favour of doing work for your clients. It's understandable that you want to do this. I mean, your clients won't be happy if you don't meet their requirements and expectations, and this can have detrimental effects in the short and long term, but with that said, you cannot lose sight of the fact that working on your business is essential if you are going to attract more of the clients that you'd love to work with in the future.

Ask yourself, if you were the client working with your business, would you be happy with the work that has been done to develop it and the attention it's been paid in the last month?

Make your business your best client and schedule time to work on it just as you would with your other clients.

Rewards

In a fun ending to the rocks, pebbles and sand demonstration, the professor pours a bottle of Budweiser into the jar, which gets soaked up by the sand. When questioned about the meaning of the beer and what it represents, the professor simply said when you get everything done in a day, there's nothing wrong in celebrating with a beer!

Get your priorities straight. Schedule your big rocks first, then your pebbles, and deal with the sand in between.

Planning for success

Networking has taught me a lot about business. One example is the value of concise and precise communication. It helps to be very specific about what you say you are looking for in those situations, and very often you are given a maximum of a single minute to get that information across.

After hearing lots of people accelerate and stress out through the last 10 seconds of their allotted time at an incoherent pace, only to have their final sentence interrupted by the buzzer, it becomes clear that people try to fit too much into the time they have.

Here's a tip for you that is applicable in many different areas of your life – including those infamous network meeting pitches.

> **When your time is limited,**
> **Then follow the 75% rule.**

If you have 60 seconds to talk about your business at a networking event, plan for 45 seconds. You'll feel way more relaxed, and as a result, you will be able to present what you want to say with emphasis on the key words, pauses where appropriate, and even the odd breath of air (always a good thing), instead of just racing through everything. The 75% rule works regardless of the time:

- For a 10-minute presentation - plan 7.5 minutes of content

- For an hour - plan 45 minutes

- For 5 minutes - plan just under 4 minutes

This is also helpful because if you end up ad-libbing, stalling or going off kilter (we've all done it under the pressure), you still have time.

Don't worry about finishing early and having nothing to say. That extra time gets easily swallowed up and rarely materialises. Even if it does appear, you can engage with the audience and answer questions - or even finish early if you're delivering training! Everyone loves an early finish!

> **"That was interesting, but I wish it had taken**
> **them longer to say it" - No-one, ever.**

You can apply the 75% rule to your scheduling, too.

- If you have 4 hours, don't try to pack 4 hours' worth of work into it. You'll inevitably get distracted at some point, and would struggle to be at your best for 4 straight hours anyway.

- If a journey should take you 45 minutes, allow at least an hour.

- If you need an hour to get ready, allow 80 minutes.

Another way to remember and apply this principle is to think of 'VAT'. Not Value Added Tax, but Valuable Additional Time. When you are estimating how long something will take to complete, simply add 'VAT' and give yourself some Valuable Additional Time.

Doing this gives you wiggle room. And who doesn't want that?

> **When you're estimating how long something will take,**
> **Then add VAT.**

Don't pack your schedule - it will only stress you out. Whether in meetings, reading, or any activity that requires you to think, it is important to remember that you are only human. In many ways, small business owners achieve incredible things; you have to in order to survive, sometimes. Nevertheless, you are still human, and if you're working hard every minute of every day, burnout will eventually catch up with you. Working harder is only ever a short-term solution - working smarter is always the answer.

As a mere human, your concentration span has its limits. For instance, when driving, people often go onto autopilot within 10 minutes. In meetings, people's minds start to drift after about 6 minutes of inactivity (ie, just listening). And in conversations with other people, people usually glance at their smartphone within 10 minutes. Unsurprisingly, the length of time that something holds your attention depends on what it is. Leisure activities can hold our attention for around half an hour, whereas work tasks tend to last only about 10 minutes before our minds drift. I tell you this so that you can be mindful of it – not to suggest that you only work in 10-minute stints. We've already covered the fact that for many reasons, 'a good hour' is ideal.

The takeaway point of all of this research is that humans aren't really designed for long bouts of intense work. It's historical. Back in the times of cavemen, activity was carried out in short, sharp bursts; pretty much resembling/following the patterns of a Big Cat. Recovery time would punctuate the end of each activity. The caveman would go out, kill his lunch, and drag it home. Then, he'd have a rest before the next burst of activity (building a fire, fighting off an aforementioned big cat, etc). It was a cycle of intense activity followed by recovery.

Fast forward a few thousand years, and we had the Industrial Revolution. People clocked in, fulfilled their role in the factory chain, and clocked out at the end of the day. Long periods of sustained activity ruled the day. The reason people could (and still can) adapt, is because this type of work is largely repetitive and doesn't require a huge amount of thinking or indeed energy. The same cannot be said for small business owners. Long hours of repetition wouldn't even scratch the surface of success.

The technological age is more about creativity and innovation, and that kind of work suits the caveman approach much better than the factory approach.

Overscheduling can be harmful. Resist the temptation to fill your calendar. There is a beauty in simplicity. Many of the world's most successful people have very minimalistic schedules. They respect their time, prioritise their own development, and keep themselves flexible enough for any big opportunities that arise.

The 2020 Pandemic (that we're still in during the time of writing this book at the start of 2021), made many people realise that many of the things they were doing on a daily basis were unnecessary. Lockdown forced people to stop travelling so much, work online as much as possible, and have more time with their loved ones (whether they liked it or not)!

In many ways it was an awful time, but in others it was a blessing. Are you able to look at your current schedule in an objective way and:

- Stop doing things that you don't really need to do?

- Do the things you need to do in a more efficient way?

- Dedicate more time to your health and your family?

If you're reading this at a time when the pandemic has long been and gone, have a think to yourself, what if everything changed tomorrow? What would suddenly be unimportant?

Why e-calendars are better than diaries

What do you use to manage your time?

An e-calendar is perfect and a diary is fine.

If you're not using either, then one thing's for sure.

Your chance of completing your day's tasks is poor.

Here's some advice that could help you a tonne.

Plan every day carefully; what gets scheduled gets done.

There are many reasons that e-calendars are more effective than diaries. Here are 4 of them:

1. You can access it pretty much anywhere, at any time, and on a number of different devices.

2. You can easily schedule repeat entries, for those things you want to do regularly.

3. You can drag and drop, including emails (which lots of people don't know).

4. You can utilise helpful apps like Calendly, which allows you to book meetings easily. Or rather, it books them for you!

I'm not saying you should definitely throw away your paper diary or planner. For many people, writing things down can be helpful in so many more ways than simply reminding them of things. Just don't rule out having an e-calendar, as well, for all the reasons I've just listed.

> **If you haven't done so already, set yourself up with an e-calendar.**

Scheduling a start time is important, of course, but setting an end time is equally as important, because when we have a realistic deadline, we generally stick to it. One thing for certain is that we can't hit a deadline we don't set, and that's one reason that meetings nearly always go on for longer than they should.

> **When you set the start time for an activity,**
> **Then set an end time for it as well.**

Look through your calendar for the next 3 days and add a deliberate finish time to every activity you have scheduled (not just the default 'hour after start time'). Make sure you share that information prior to the activity with any other people involved.

A common misconception is the idea that a crammed schedule is a productive one. Quite often the opposite is true. Sometimes we get held up, for a million different reasons, and to allow for that, and to protect our mental health at the same time, it's advisable to have some wiggle room between tasks.

But doesn't that just result in loads of dead time between tasks, you may ask? Not necessarily.

To make use of an idea from Stephen Covey's book, 'Seven Habits of Highly Effective People', for most of us, there are some tasks that are 'urgent' (time-bound, like meetings), and some tasks that are 'important but not urgent' (just need to be done at some point before a deadline, like a report). My suggestion to you is that your time-bound tasks are carefully positioned as the skeleton of your day (with minimal travel, avoiding busy times/routes where possible), and the other tasks are slotted in between. That way, if everything goes to plan, you'll get everything done, and if it doesn't, we can reschedule one of the 'important but not urgent' tasks elsewhere.

The To-Do List

A common tool used by people in business and in life is the to-do list. Also known as the graveyard of tasks that never get done. Why is it that the tasks towards the bottom of a to-do list can linger for so long – sitting patiently in line, whilst other tasks constantly cut in front of them?

It's simple, really - there's no urgency in a to-do list. With no plan of when, where and how you're going to do it, there's a good chance that the tricky things you don't really want to do will just sit there on the list, out of mind, and out of action.

Multiply this by a million for a special kind of task: The ones with no deadline at all. The things that you should do because they'll make things better in the future, but nobody is pressuring you for them to be done. Well, no deadline = no action.

There is a common saying, 'A dream without a plan is just a wish.' The same can be said for to-do lists.

A to-do list is a capture tool, not an action tool. It's great for getting that list of things out of your head so that you don't forget anything, but it's only really when it is scheduled with a date, time and place that it becomes real. After all, you don't miss meetings and appointments because you're committed to them, so we should treat important tasks in the same way.

When writing your to-do list (if you must write one):

- Get everything out of your head and onto the list. Don't worry too much about how, just get it down there.

- Label each item on the list as either 'Do', 'Delegate', 'Schedule' or 'Bin'.

- Take immediate action in response. Either do it now, delegate it to someone else, schedule a fixed time when you'll do it in your calendar, or throw it in the bin!

To-do lists are a great way to record everything that needs to be done, but they are lousy at getting you to actually do them.

Your mind is like a computer

If you've ever had multiple tabs open on your computer, you've probably found that it runs slower. In a similar way, your mind can get overwhelmed when you have too many 'tabs' open in your working memory.

You may need to remember to call someone, email someone and submit some accounts, but then somebody calls you and you remember mid-call that you need to do a couple of personal errands. Things build up and, not surprisingly, you can't operate at anything close to your potential.

Use everything you've learned so far and close some tabs.

If you ever feel overwhelmed by how many tabs you have open, talk about it. Maybe someone can help you, or maybe you just have to tell someone you need a little bit longer to get things done (then you can schedule it).

> **When you have lots of things to do,**
> **Then make a list and schedule everything into your calendar.**

When things we need to do are building up in our mind, stress increases in line with it. When they are scheduled with a specific date, place and time, that stress lifts straight off.

Energy

Energy flow is an important factor to consider if you are going to get maximum productivity from your day.

There is a book called 'Eat that Frog' by Brian Tracy, which helps us to avoid procrastination by completing the task that we dread the most, first. He quotes Mark Twain in saying, "If the first thing you do each morning is to *eat a live frog*, you can go through the day with the satisfaction of knowing that this is probably the worst thing that is going to happen to you all day."

This is popular advice for people who are at their best in the morning, because they'd get their biggest task completed early, and at a time when they are feeling happiest, healthiest and most productive. They simply have more energy.

A book by Dan Pink entitled 'When', explains how energy flow is largely down to our circadian rhythms. Most people (not all) have an energy peak in the morning, a trough after lunch, and then a recovery in the late afternoon. The important take away here is that we can achieve our best results when we marry up our most important tasks and decisions with the times in the day that our energy levels are at their highest, and use the times when our energy is lower for the more repetitive, process type tasks that don't require as much brain power.

In schools, certain subjects are positioned at specific times of the day. This is because it is believed that most people are more logical in the morning and more creative in the afternoon.

At what point of the day do you find your energy levels are generally at their highest? Bear it in mind.

Do you think there are certain tasks in your life that would be better done in the morning and others in the afternoon?

For example, is there a time that is usually more successful for calling clients, or a quiet point in the day where you can normally get stuck into some paperwork?

Of course, the time you select may be different each time. Just choose the time when you are personally at your best to do your most important tasks.

When you have an important task to complete,
Then schedule it for the time when you expect
you'll be at your best.

Level Two

Block 8

Discipline

All in

Everyone wants to have won, but few are willing to go through the pain of becoming a winner.

Your vision is set and you know that if you stretch yourself you can achieve it. You've created a plan with milestones, and have made commitments for when you will reach each one. All you need now is the discipline to see it through...

Labelling

A few years ago, my wife and I went through the approval process as Foster Carers. A key part of it was a series of interviews that drilled down into the experiences we had as children and how they played a role in the choices we made in adulthood, and the people we ultimately became. Prior to that I didn't fully appreciate how seemingly meaningless things can turn out to be so influential in shaping your mindset, but it was an eye-opener to say the least.

I realised that labelling is really powerful. People really do live up (or down) to the expectations that are placed on them. For children in care, overcoming experiences of abuse, rejection and a multitude of other things presents a heart-breaking challenge in creating a world for them where they can expect more for themselves.

Looking back at my own school life, a moment in high school made a lot of sense to me. I think it was fairly early on, maybe the first year, and we were put into different 'sets' for each class. Put simply, the top set was for the more advanced kids, the bottom set was for the lower achievers who perhaps needed more support, and the middle set was for everyone else. Within my main friendship group, most people were put into the higher sets and a few in the lower sets. I was placed bang in the middle set for most things (but in the top sets for languages).

At the time I didn't think much of it, and just got on with my lessons and did as I was told. When I think about it, we all really lived up to the expectations that came with being in a particular set. The ones in the top sets got the best grades, the middle set got average grades and the lower set got the lowest grades. To be honest, I never felt particularly challenged at school and whenever I saw some of the work my top set friends were doing, it honestly didn't seem to be beyond my capabilities either.

I just did what I was told, finished the work that was put in front of me and got average grades as a result. The mindset that I'd adopted at school saw me continue to achieve average grades throughout College and University.

One theory is that those teachers were exactly right to put us in the sets they did at the start and set work that was entirely appropriate. Another is that the expectations that were set by labelling people as top, middle or bottom set, encouraged a mindset of what could – and should - be achieved. There's no way of knowing what would've happened if we'd all have been placed in different sets, but in the last few years in particular I've really started thinking about it. As an adult learner, I have always had a 'top set' mentality and that does make me aware about the power of labelling. I've also proved to do quite well, too!

Of course, everyone's situation is different and I'm not for a second comparing my happy childhood in a nice area with loving and supportive parents to that of a child who has entered the care system and potentially had the most traumatic or unstable of childhoods through no fault of their own. What I *am* saying, however is that the underlying principle of labelling rings true for everyone, and it is natural to meet the expectations placed on you by yourself and others.

What do you expect for yourself?

- When you label yourself as 'a terrible procrastinator', you create an environment that gives you permission to miss deadlines.
- When you set three morning alarms, you set yourself up to start your day with procrastination before it even starts.
- When you write things on your To-Do list without a deadline, you make it easy to delay doing it until tomorrow, or next week, or never.

How about this...

- Would you change your ways if you started labelling yourself as punctual and took pride in being early?
- Would you get up with the first alarm if you knew it was the only one?
- If you scheduled things in your calendar would you be more likely to actually do them?

The answer to these three questions is almost certainly yes, which shows that the first challenge in defeating procrastination is to develop a mindset of productivity. Start labelling yourself in a more helpful way!

Procrastination

Procrastination is often the butt of jokes about time management, so I'll start by getting that out of my system...

"My partner has a big problem with my procrastination. I told her we'd discuss it next week."

"I'm finally going to stop procrastinating, starting tomorrow!"

"Name a better procrastinator than me... I'll wait!"

Joking aside, procrastination is a prolific time thief and a very common challenge that people would like to overcome. Thankfully, procrastination doesn't have to be a permanent feature of your life, but it does need you to understand it and for you to take responsibility for adopting a more productive mindset to defeat it.

Waiting for the right time

How many things have you delayed something because it's not the right time?

Sometimes, there are legitimate reasons why something has to wait. If you're planning out the alphabet and the opportunity for the letter 'J' comes up when you're only at the letter 'B' stage, there's a good argument to say you should wait a little bit longer before going for it. I know there are more relatable and realistic examples to give, here, but I don't want to zone in on anyone's life choices!

Timing is important in everything you do, and getting the right things in your life at the right time is imperative to your success. But very often, there isn't a logical reason to delay doing things that you know will take you closer to your goals. If you're human, and I assume you are, you probably have a mind that tries to persuade you that you should do things that you want to do and avoid things that you don't want to do, or you're waiting for all of the stars to align before you take action. The problem is, it will never be the perfect time. There will always be a reason *not* to do something that takes your time and some level of commitment.

If you can't pinpoint a really good reason not to do something, it may well actually be the right time to do it *now*. None of us are getting any younger, and if the pandemic during which this book was written proves anything, we have no idea what's going to happen tomorrow.

Get MAD about procrastination

A good strategy for beating Procrastination is to keep calm and... get MAD.

Let me explain. By MAD I mean that you should make sure that these three key things are in place:

Motivation - Be clear about why you are doing what you are trying to do. Is it something you're trying to move *closer to*, like a nice holiday, a new car, or an early finish? Or is it something you want to move *away from*, like an angry client, a nightmare boss, or the disappointed look on your family's faces as you get home late again? Keep your motivation in mind. When the why is strong enough... the how becomes easier.

Accountability – Who is holding you accountable for doing something on time? It's wise to have an Accountabilibuddy (I love that word!) for important tasks, and it is important to select the best person for each task. Your partner or kids will probably be good at holding you accountable to spending quality time with them, but probably not great at the work-based accountability, as they will often have a conflict of interests in wanting you to be doing LESS work. For certain things, a colleague, customer or fellow mentee in a coaching group will be more effective. Select the best person and make them a promise they can hold you to.

Deadlines - Parkinson's Law says that things will expand to fill the space they are allowed. When you have a 3-month deadline for something it's too easy to wait 2 and a half months to start (just ask students!). In general, people overestimate what they can achieve in a day and underestimate what they can achieve in a year, so it's advisable to set mini-deadlines as milestones towards achieving the main goal. Get your Accountabilibuddy to hold you to your promises to meet your mini-deadlines.

If you get MAD, you can defeat procrastination!

I know what I need to do!

Isn't it frustrating when you know what you need to do but you just don't do it? It usually happens on tasks that you don't want to do. You don't enjoy them and the idea of doing them just makes your brain go into overdrive searching for a distraction as an excuse not to do it.

They say that knowledge is power, but I have a problem with that as a statement, because I know loads of people who have lots of knowledge but don't use it, and they are not as successful (or powerful, I guess) as other people I know with far less knowledge but a lot more common sense.

Knowledge, it seems, is powerless without application.

So why don't we do things that are easy for us to do? Well, probably because they're also easy to *not* do.

To combat this, you need to ensure two things:

- That the benefit of having done it will be bigger than the comfort of not doing it.

- That the pain of having not done it is greater than the discomfort of actually doing it.

The MAD principle we have just covered depends on you having motivation to draw upon, here, but sometimes you just don't care enough about something, even though you know it needs to be done.

In cases like these, you really need to re-focus on the reasons why performing a task will be beneficial for you, even if that simply means you can rid it from your schedule and never have to look at it again. If you need a boost to get it done, make a promise to someone who can hold you accountable for getting it done by an agreed time.

Gimme 5

More often than not, the hardest thing about beating procrastination is getting started. There are so many reasons why it seems better to delay doing a task until later:

- You're not sure what to do first.
- There are various ways you could go with the task and you're not sure which one to choose.
- You'll feel better if you make a drink and something to eat first.
- One last check of your emails and social media notifications will let you reset and focus.
- You can't be bothered doing it yet.
- You didn't sleep well last night so it's probably not going to be your best effort.

When I was training for the London Marathon, I knew that I needed to follow a 16-week training programme in order to be properly prepared for race day. In my mind it was clear what I needed to do. This was something I had signed up for myself and wanted to do.

There were, however, times when it was raining, windy and cold when I was due to go out for a training run. In those moments, I loved the idea of having *done* the run, but found it hard to be enthusiastic about actually *doing* it. My mind was very creative and innovative when trying to persuade me to skip the run and choose a more comfortable option instead.

- Too cold / wet / windy.
- I don't feel great.
- There's plenty of other things I could do instead.
- I can do a bit extra tomorrow.
- A day off won't hurt.

It was important to make a start, and for me this came way before taking that first step outside. It was about getting the running kit and trainers on. I knew that once I'd done that, I'd feel (and look) pretty stupid if I didn't actually go on the run.

Although I'd often be soaked to the bone returning from one of those runs, and wind-burned to within an inch of my life, I'd feel good about having done it in the short term and the long term, given the focus of my end goal (competing in the London Marathon). Getting started is sometimes the biggest challenge you will face in getting certain tasks done, so 'Gimme 5' is a technique that can help you do that and form an important part of your mindset of productivity.

How does it work? It's a simple concept of committing to five minutes on the task. Whatever form that takes, it doesn't really matter. Just make a start and work on it for 5 minutes. After 5 minutes you have full permission to stop and do whatever you want to do instead, whether that's making a brew, checking social media, or going for a shower.

That may sound counter-productive, but it actually works, because whilst there may be the odd occasion that you do indeed take up the offer of stopping after 5 minutes, the vast majority of times you won't actually do that. Making a start is the hardest bit.

With my running, I never stopped after 5 minutes. I'd have felt ridiculous doing that. Once I'd started, I carried on and finished the run. The same principle applies with work. If you need to do a load of invoices, just Gimme 5 and start on the first one. If you need to make some sales calls, create a job advert or get to work on a project, just Gimme 5 and open up that document.

> **When you can't get motivated to start,**
> **Then just Gimme 5.**

'Doing' is very different to 'done'.

Whilst getting started is often the most difficult challenge, it isn't the only battle we face in the war against procrastination.

How many horror movies have you seen that feature a scene where our hero finally appears to have killed the blood-thirsty, evil villain of the piece who has been tormenting them for the entire movie? They breathe a sigh of relief, drop their gun or knife or whatever, and take their eyes off the ball (or in this case the axe wielding maniac), only to find that their nemesis isn't in fact dead at all, but still very much alive and very much a threat. Every time, you shout something at the screen, like "Shoot him in the head! Make sure he's dead!" or similar, but they never seem to listen, do they?

It's the same with procrastination. Task abandonment is the unexpected second wave of attack that comes from your failure to finish the job. Just like in those movies, you've got to nail the coffin shut when you get the chance!

Keeping on track can be difficult when you want something to be the best it can possibly be. Take social media posts for your marketing, for instance. You finally get round to writing something, but then you write the first sentence and delete it and start again. You switch a few words around and it still doesn't feel perfect. You write it again, and again, and again before you start to wonder whether social media is the best way for you to promote yourself at all. You thought you'd beaten procrastination by making a start, but find yourself locked in a battle that can see you spend hours tapping away on your laptop without ever actually posting anything!

This form of procrastination is often referred to as 'perfection paralysis'. You want to get something perfect, but as a result, you don't get it done at all.

An important thing to remember is that 'doing' doesn't pay the bills, but 'done' certainly gets you closer. Get into the habit of finishing the job without worrying if it is perfect. Get it to the stage where you could send it and it would be OK, then you can edit later if you want to. My wife, the copywriter, is glaring at me right now...

For relatively small tasks, it's a good idea to get into the habit of finishing what you start before moving onto anything else. So, when opening your mail... open it, deal with it, then file it or bin it. Done.

If a task is too big to do in one sitting, then break it down into smaller pieces and treat them as individual tasks. Not only does this help remove the feeling of overwhelm that can cause you to procrastinate, but it also allows you to stick to the habit of finishing what you start.

> **When you start a small individual task,**
> **Then make sure you finish it in the same sitting.**

Having an accountability partner - an 'Accountabilibuddy' as I've already referred to them as - definitely helps with all of this. They're like fire alarms!

Sound the accountability alarm!

If you're a responsible home-owner, you will more than likely have thought about fire safety in your home at some point. Amongst other things, you'll have smoke alarms, an escape plan, and a routine of making sure things are switched off at night.

Why do you do this? Because you know that if a fire started during the night it would cause devastation to your home and risk the lives of you and your family. The scariest thing is that you could inhale lethal fumes without even realising that anything was wrong. So, you take precautions including the installation of alarms that will warn you of potential problems; hopefully early enough for you to do something about them before it's too late.

Having an accountability partner works in the same way. They protect you and your goals like your fire alarm protects you and your home.

If installed correctly, if you haven't done what you said you would do by a certain time, your accountability partner will recognise that something is wrong and sound the alarm.

They know that your goals are in danger of burning to the ground if they don't make you act quickly, so they make loud and uncomfortable noises, and it works. Nobody likes the sound of a fire alarm and nobody likes to be told they are failing and not going to achieve their goals, so you take action to protect your home from fire - and your goals from failure.

This is why it is essential to select the right person to hold you accountable. If they're too quiet and easy to ignore they won't be very effective. You need someone who can make you take action immediately. Someone you really don't want to let down (or get on the wrong side of).

For work things, your customers are often enough to hold you accountable. They'll certainly let you know if you don't do what you promised by a deadline, that's for sure.

For relationships, your family are well placed. Try telling them you're all going on a lovely day out and then cancel it at the last minute. See how well that goes down.

For process-based things, it is useful to use a coach. This applies to working on your business, and also to working on your health. Both are processes that are under the radar because they don't have anyone shouting for them to happen immediately, but they are essential things that develop (with positive or negative effects) over time. If a coach's role is to hold you accountable, they have a vested interest in your success if they want to continue working with you. Whether it's a business coach, a personal trainer or another specialist, if you select the right person it can be extremely effective in ensuring you do the things you need to do in order to reach your everyday milestones and bigger picture goals.

A smart decision?

Make your bed.

That was the well-documented advice given at the University of Texas Commencement Address in 2014 by Navy SEAL Commander, Admiral William H McRaven. He spoke about starting the day well and then building on it from that bed-making point.

The SEALS famously get up very early each morning, and certainly don't get as much sleep as I'm sure they'd like to in achieving this. A lesson we can take from them is that it's more about *how* you get up than when you get up.

If you struggle to get up in the mornings and always want to hit the snooze button, you may find the following technique useful.

The sound of your alarm was designed to wake you up from even the deepest slumber, so it's no surprise that it isn't usually nice to listen to! Whilst your body is in shock from the sound of the alarm, your mind adopts some kind of 'lawyer' mode and immediately starts to build a case of all the reasons why you shouldn't get up yet.

- It's cold!

- I'm tired!

- I don't need time for a shower after all!

- This bed is so comfy!

And then it presents a settlement offer: Let's just have a few more minutes. Bliss.

You know you should get up, but your mind will do everything it possibly can to try and talk you out of it. If you hit that snooze button you might think it's making it easier for you but usually it isn't. It's just a bit more time for your mind to line up more reasons to persuade you to press it again. For many people this is an important Time Habit to break.

It starts with your perception of the whole process of getting up in the morning.

Zig Ziglar pointed out that the term 'alarm' has negative connotations in itself. Alarms are generally warnings of bad things, but we want everything a new day brings to be an opportunity, not a warning, so let's rename your alarm clock. Zig suggests 'opportunity clock' but you can go with whatever works for you. I imagine some of you are rolling your eyes at that example.

In line with the 'make your bed' idea, creating a precedent for doing things 'right first time' can help you to override the inevitable reluctance to get up and focus your mind. Deep down you know that an extra 10 minutes isn't really going to make things better, but it could almost definitely make you late – or at least underprepared.

Add to that the fact that you are programming your mind to make a decision between starting your day with a win or a loss, and it's becoming easier to make the decision to start the day off positively. I hope!

I promise you, when you get out of bed you won't feel any worse than if you did it 10 minutes later. The only difference is that you will have 10 minutes more time to get yourself ready for the day, and also feel a little bit proud of yourself that you started the day with the win that you had promised yourself that you would.

With a mindset of doing things 'right first time' and a success to start your day with, hopefully you can continue to do things right first time throughout the day.

When you set the alarm (or whatever you want to call it), listen to the sound that will play and say to yourself, 'right first time'. If you still don't quite trust yourself, place it out of reach so that you will physically have to get out of bed to switch it off.

When that sound goes off you will make the connection in your mind, remember those three words and make a decision:

Am I going to have a day of doing things right first time, or am I not?

There aren't many people who enjoy wasting their time doing things wrong and re-doing them, so hopefully that question will get the desired response from you.

It may feel like a challenge at the time, but it's actually simple – and it really works. Well, it does for me, anyway. Give it a try, and if it works, start a streak. How many days in a row can you get up first time without giving in to the urge to hit the snooze button?

If you do it once, you'll have made a good start to the day. Do it twice and you're on a streak. 10 times in a row and you won't want to break that streak. 20? You're well on the way to having established an effective Time Habit.

> **When you agree to doing something,**
> **Then commit to getting it 'Right First Time'.**

That first step of actually getting up is usually the hardest one, but once you're up there are still plenty of early morning time thieves to be aware of. The prime suspect for most people is the smart phone, loaded with hours of news, updates, alerts and goodness knows what else that have built up since you went to sleep. It's tempting to have a quick look, but it is very easy to get drawn in.

The problem with smart phones and social media is that they are packed with other people's priorities, and that can hi-jack your mind and steal your focus away from your own priorities. There are undoubtedly positive things on social media, but I bet you can't look at it for more than a few minutes without seeing something that annoys or concerns you! Is that the best way to start your day?

It can be a good idea to resist the urge to look at your phone first thing in the morning, and instead take a couple of minutes to wake up naturally and start your day in a more positive way. Take a moment to think about what you want to achieve in the day ahead, and then get out of bed and make it happen. Your social media will still be there later when you check it on your own terms having first achieved the most important things you wanted to do with your morning.

I feel I should point out in this section that if you're going to master your time, it's important to start your day well. It is, however, important to remember that you're starting **your** day, not someone else's. There are endless online and book-writing 'gurus' who will tell you that the key to their success is getting up at 4am, going for a 10-mile run, or eating raw eggs from an old clog. Sometimes it can seem ridiculous, but if it works for them, good for them. Really, the only ridiculous thing is that other people force themselves to copy the same rituals in the hope that this will be *their* perfect start to the day as well.

Your day should start in **your** way. Try lots of different things, by all means, until you find what works best for you. Pay attention to how energetic you feel after certain actions or tasks, and replace anything that zaps your energy with things that launch you into your day most effectively. That should be your priority first thing in the morning.

Multi-tasking

You can't multi-task.

It's true.

If you want proof, try this exercise:

Count out loud in multiples of 3 as quickly as you can. 3,6,9,12 etc.

Now, say the alphabet out loud as quickly as you can. A,B,C,D,E etc.

Both pretty easy things to do, I'm sure you'll agree? Now, try and multi-task both things.

3,A,6,B,9,C etc.

For most people this demonstrates how much harder the brain has to work when it has to think about two things simultaneously, even when the tasks are both fairly simple when carried out independently of each other. So, next time you have two things to do that both require your concentration, remember that you will be far more efficient if you do them one at a time, rather than both together.

Level Two

The 3Cs

Clarity, Communication and Consistency

Over the years, I've had the good fortune to work with many different types of businesses – big and small, corporate and creative. During that time, I've spotted a pattern that every single one of them follows. I call it 'The 3Cs'.

The businesses (and individuals for that matter) that are the most effective in achieving their goals always have all three of the 3Cs, and of the businesses that are struggling, there is always at least one of the 3Cs missing. Those Cs are

Clarity, Communication and Consistency.

Clarity

Where are you going? What is your vision and how are you going to achieve it? Having a clear plan will make it far more likely that you will achieve the things that you want.

You need to be clear about what you do, the benefits of what you do, and how you actively do it. So many people aren't clear enough about this and it leads to a real lack of clarity for everyone involved.

In addition, your terms should be clear so that people know what to expect. Your colleagues should know how you work, you should be in agreement with your suppliers about service and payment terms, and your customers need to know what they can expect from you and what is expected from them.

Employees are often criticised for 'not caring' as much about the business as the owner does. If that is the case, there is probably a disconnect between the persons goals and the goals of the organisation. Everyone works for themselves, ultimately. The best approach is to find the alignment between the two, so that an employee can achieve *their* goals by helping the organisation to achieve its own goals in the process.

In practice, this can take the form of a Personal Development Plan. Just as you would for your business, you can help your employee to create a vision of where they'd like to be and how they will get there. Maybe they want to save for a deposit on a house so need more money, or maybe they want to learn new skills. Whatever they want, if you can help them to plan for it they will know that you care about them as a person. If their plans align with those of the business, then they'll definitely start to 'care more' about the business. And if they don't align? Well, it's better to find out now rather than later. You can download a PDP template from www.27andahalf.co.uk if you feel it would be helpful.

A clear message can shape the shared thinking of a group of people, which is great when you need a team to achieve a goal together. For example, questions like 'Will it make the boat go faster?', 'How would it look to the customer?' and 'Is this replicable?' can act as decision making themes that over time become a key part of the development and culture of an organisation. The boat will be a metaphor for the chosen aspect of your business, obviously.

Every aspect of your business model needs to be sound and clear. Don't leave anything to chance. Crunch the numbers, create a cash flow forecast, and make decisions accordingly.

Communication

People always have questions - and that's a good thing. Well, it is when you can answer them!

The problem with unanswered questions is that people tend to draw their own conclusions, and in my experience, those conclusions are often inaccurate, unhelpful and potentially damaging.

With so many potential questions, your availability should be made clear. Without guidance, people will make their own rules, so it's important to communicate with them if you want to avoid that.

When is it OK for people to pop their head around your door? How can they book a meeting with you? Apps like Calendly can be great, but without effective parameters applied to them they can cause more problems than they solve. As ever, the software is only as effective as its user.

There are many ways of communicating with individuals and groups, and the skill lies in being able to select the most effective one in a given situation. For example, sending an email or an instant message is great for sharing information quickly, but if it could be misinterpreted in any way then a phone call is probably better. Better still would be face to face, but that might not be convenient, so perhaps a video call is the happy medium. For general communication you may choose a newsletter, and of course there are meetings, but it is advisable to keep them to a minimum.

The 5-minute one-to-one is a useful tool. This is a regular meeting between you and your employee to establish what's going well, how we could make it even better, and the commitments and actions needed between now and the next meeting. The actual meeting only takes 5 minutes because the answers are given on a shared document, which can be downloaded from www.27andahalf.co.uk, if you need a template. I highly recommend this style of meeting as a great use of time, whether in person or online.

Communication is key in delegation. Lots of people struggle with delegation, by the way. They hate it when people try to pass work onto them, as it makes them feel uncomfortable and used. On the other side of it, lots of people find it difficult to delegate tasks to others in the first place. They hate it when people dump extra work onto *them*, so they feel uncomfortable doing the same thing to someone else. Unfortunately, delegation is necessary if you are going to protect your own time and avoid doing everything yourself.

Dale Carnegie's timeless communication advice is my best suggestion here: 'Talk in terms of the other person's interests'. If you're delegating, this frames the task in a way that is of benefit to the other person rather than simply being a favour to you. This has to be genuine, though – not mere manipulation through false niceties, promises you can't keep, or making someone feel bad if they don't want to do it. A conversation may follow, so be respectful. Ask yourself if you're asking too much, but also remember, sometimes what you're asking someone to do is actually their job in the first place...

Communication is vital with clients and customers. It can be frightening to ask for feedback, especially if you aren't sure how positive it will be. It's as if not asking will make the possibility of the client being unhappy go away. It won't. If they're not happy, the sooner you know about it, the better. In fact, a good habit to get into is asking the 10/10 question on a regular basis.

'How happy are you with our current working relationship on a scale of 0-10?'

If the answer is 10/10, it's a great time to ask for an introduction to someone else that they know - or at least a testimonial. Strike while the iron is hot! If the answer is 9/10 or lower, you can ask them how you can make it a 10/10 and strive to achieve it.

Consistency

Hell hath no fury like a person who feels unfairly treated, and one thing that is guaranteed to make people feel something isn't fair is when they are criticised for something that others have previously done without any issues.

Consistency creates a degree of predictability that enables people to use their initiative. Without it, people feel unsure about what they are supposed to do in any given situation - and that leads to lack of confidence, inefficiencies, and unhappiness. It's easy to identify when a business has consistency or not by the way its people act.

It is also essential in the process of developing habits. When you do things consistently, other people know what they can expect from you - and you know what you can expect from yourself. Aristotle once said (I believe), 'We are what we repeatedly do', and so when you expect certain things of yourself, you can develop them into habits. When that consistency spreads throughout a team, it creates the kind of culture that the very best organisations are built upon.

The new 'E' myth

Clarity, Communication and Consistency, you say? So, if I apply that principle to social media, that must mean that I must post every day...?

Not exactly.

There is a misconception with social media that you need to post all day, every day. You don't.

Is it important to build relationships with people?

Yes.

Should you showcase your successes, ideas and offers, so that people can see the value of what you share with them?

Absolutely.

Can we build a strong and credible brand presence through effective use of social media?

No doubt about it.

But, as with everything, you should probably post in moderation...

How often should you post?

I think the answer depends on how much you have got to say that people will actually want to read.

That may seem obvious, but so many people post for the sake of posting in the hope of building a presence, and this actually waters down the quality of their posts considerably.

In addition, there is a misconception that if someone is posting regularly, then it must be because they are ridiculously busy and wildly successful (probably because their posts will literally tell you that). But if you think about it, they must have a fair amount of free time on their hands if they're posting on social media all day!

How much does it cost?

Another misconception with social media is that it is free. This is simply not the case. Although there are no fees to open and use a standard account, that doesn't account for the time you spend on it. If you think about the time it takes you to think up, write and edit a LinkedIn post, for example, and multiply that by the number of days you want to post, you can then apply your hourly rate as determined in the 'Value your time' section of the book. That's what it's costing you. This is before we calculate the time taken to respond to messages and to post comments, of course. Or the time taken when you invariably drift across the platform to engage with something else entirely...

If it's costing money, you'll be tempted to put a decent call to action in there to make sure that your post makes a sale, but this is another area to tread carefully within. The posts that tend to do the best in brand building are the ones that are interesting and engaging without looking like a sales post. When people read those posts they'll be tempted to check you out and see who you are. Marketing at its finest.

There have been so many times I've seen a post that I enjoyed reading until the final sentence, where shoehorned in is a sentence that states something like, 'So, if you need any X then contact us and we will Y.' It turns me off the entire thing. Nobody likes to be pitched to. If you're going to sell, just be plain about it.

There are probably a lot of sales and marketing gurus that would disagree with me on this, but in my opinion going for engagement when you have something great to say instead of going for the kill every day to fill space is the best approach when thinking about getting a return on the time you put into your marketing.

The 6-month rule

What does your home screen look like on your computer? Is it tidy or is it full of random things all over the place? How about your email inbox? It is all in order or have you got thousands of unread emails?

There is a lot of evidence to suggest that these things have an impact on the way you thrive (or not) in your business. Whether or not you buy into that idea is up to you, but either way, decluttering your homescreen and inbox can only be a positive thing for focus, ease and clarity – three things that only ever give you more time to play with.

You can do the same thing in all areas of your life. Less clutter in your environment and in your mind will make you more organised, more productive, and less stressed.

Why not try the 6-month rule... If you haven't looked at it, used it, or referenced it in the last 6 months, get rid of it. Obviously, there are certain exceptions that you may need to make, but for most things it is achievable.

Select the right type of meeting

Before you select the 'right type of meeting' to have with your customers, colleagues or peers, the first consideration is, do you really need to have a meeting at all? Would a phone call or email suffice?

If a meeting is what you need, so be it.

So, now consider who needs to be there. It is sometimes tempting to invite the whole team to a meeting, but this is rarely a good idea. Generally speaking, the higher we increase the quantity of people in a conversation, not only does the cost of the meeting rise (with hourly pay, opportunity cost, and maybe increased facilities), but the further we reduce the quality of the conversation for each of them, because each person will have less time to interact.

It's a good idea to keep meetings to only the people who need to contribute or make a decision within them. Updates for everyone else can be shared in alternative ways that are more convenient at a later time. It should go without saying that you need to be fair in who you invite. Don't just cut out people for the sake of it.

By sending a clear meeting agenda with objectives to all invitees, we give them the opportunity to prepare for maximum value contribution. Giving everyone the chance to do any pre-reading of relevant information makes the meeting much more time-efficient by allowing it to be focused more on making decisions than on having discussions. By the same token, they may also suggest that they might not be able to contribute to all or part of the meeting, and request to be excused or join late/leave early.

Meetings are often all lumped together and treated the same, but there are many types of meeting and each one has its place. The most common type of meeting is the sit-down meeting, and if we want to share documentation or paperwork, it's quite effective.

Sometimes, a sit-down meeting is not the best option. Here are 3 alternative types of meeting to consider:

1. The virtual meeting - Brilliant when a few people who know each other are based in different places. The biggest benefit is convenience, as it saves everyone the travel time, and there are added benefits such as the ability to record meetings, demonstrate certain things on-location, and screen share. Some people find it harder to make the same connection online, but it is a great option in many situations.

2. The standing meeting - It's easy to get settled in a sit-down meeting, virtually or in-person, with a coffee and a nice comfortable chair, and this can encourage meetings to last longer than they need to. When we want to make a quick decision on something, a standing meeting is usually efficient. Meet, make the decision, and move on.

3. The walking meeting - In emotive and creative topics, walking meetings have been shown to encourage openness, creativity and honesty. The main reason for this, aside from the nice fresh air, is that when we are side by side with someone it creates a very different dynamic than when we are face-to-face with each other. It's calmer, more relaxed, and feels less formal. From a time perspective, it can be good to plan the length of the route you walk to match the time that you want the meeting to last.

Whichever option we choose, preparation is important. Every meeting should have a clear agenda outlining the start time, desired outcomes, and the end time. It should also include relevant information that will allow attendees to be prepared. When we set clear expectations for meetings, people are very clear about how things are to run, and from experience, those who have experienced ineffective meetings in the past are very supportive and grateful for the focus and structure going forward.

Virtual meetings have become commonplace in recent times, initially out of necessity and then out of convenience as people got more familiar with the technology. Now that they are more commonplace, there are far fewer obstacles to virtual meetings than there were previously. For anyone who still gets nervous at the thought of talking to a camera, it is useful to consider this:

'It's not about perfection. It's about connection.'

No matter how many people are in the meeting, talk as if it is just to the one person in the meeting that you feel most comfortable speaking with. Speak calmly and clearly, and treat the camera as if it is the eyes of the person you are speaking to. You wouldn't stare intently into their eyes if you were with them in person, so don't do it online either. Just make sure you get regular 'eye contact' with the camera as you would naturally do with a person.

Other than standard meeting preparations, your tick list for meeting online should include:

- **Hardware**: Make sure your computer, camera and microphone are of sufficient quality for your needs. The built-in camera and microphone on a laptop are usually fine, but as with anything in the world of tech, you can upgrade from there to suit your budget.
- **Software**: Get familiar with the platform that the meeting is to be hosted on. There are various options, each with minor differences and quirks, and some require a download in advance. You'll want

to be confident with how to join the meeting, so be ready to switch your camera on and unmute yourself as a minimum requirement.

- **Environment**: Position yourself with good lighting (preferably facing natural light), a professional background, and the camera at eye-level. Shut the cat out of the room, if humanly possible. I'm speaking from bad experience!

Great preparation, along with the most appropriate meeting type, is a recipe for success for meetings.

The 'MEET sandwich' approach can help you to get the most out of all types of meeting, now that you're ready to go.

The MEET sandwich

Fact: Most people hate meetings. The small talk, the late start, the stragglers, the disapprovers, the glass-half-fullers, the doom-and-gloomers, the death by PowerPoint, the brown nosing, the AOB.

Basically, people hate pretty much everything about meetings, and it's down to two main reasons.

1. They're not planned well enough.

2. They're not delivered well enough.

Meetings can be very necessary, though, and so when you need to have one, it should flow like a great story - with a good start, an engaging middle, and a conclusive end.

> **The main problem with the beginning and the end of your meetings is... they're too far apart.**

It might surprise you to learn that the secret to planning a successful meeting lies in a sandwich. Equally, you might be nodding your head and thinking, 'finally there's something that makes perfect sense in this book - a sandwich is the answer to every problem'. I won't judge you either way.

Let me explain, though.

Sandwiches, in general, need a slice of bread at the top, and another at the bottom to give the whole thing structure and keep it in place. Without either slice, the contents would spill everywhere and create a mess.

It's the same with meetings.

The way we start gives structure to the content of the meeting, and the way we finish makes sure we achieve what we wanted to without any spillage.

Meetings and sandwiches are surprisingly similar.

Have you ever found yourself in the middle of a meeting that you don't really know the purpose of, with no signs of light at the end of the tunnel? Of course you have. It's not an enjoyable experience, and it's normally preceded by a rubbish start that lacked focus and lost control.

I like a lovely butty for my lunch just as much as the next man, but if you get one that's been thrown together at the last minute with random leftovers - and the bread is a bit iffy - there's nothing worse, is there?

Just a little bit more preparation can turn something to endure into something to enjoy.

First things first then, how can you start a meeting in the most effective way?

Start with the end in mind. What are the desired outcomes of the meeting, and what time do we want to achieve them by? If every meeting you have starts with clarification of these two things, I guarantee they'll improve instantly.

Be bold, break the meeting into manageable chunks, and clearly communicate the plan. You are running this meeting – the meeting shouldn't be running *you*.

"Welcome everyone. You've all confirmed receipt of the pre-reading about today's topic and had time to think about it. We want to have made a decision on Z in 30 minutes time, after we've considered the determining factors X and Y. So, we'll spend 10 mins summarising X, 10 mins on Y, and then wrap up and make our final decision. In the interest of everyone's time we will stick to the script, so please don't be offended when I say it's time to move on."

Immediately, there's a structure. Everyone is focused in knowing they may be called on for something, and they can also see the finish line, which is always a brilliant incentive. We are in for a good meeting.

> **When you are starting a meeting,**
> **Then confirm the desired outcomes and finish time.**

What could go wrong? Oh yeah, Amelia is going to be there, or as she's better known, 'Me-Me'. She will want to make everything about her and take us off topic.

Every meeting has a Me-Me, so here's a little bonus tool: Post-Its. It's the thing that protects your MEET sandwich.

"On the table is a stack of Post-It Notes. If a thought pops into your head and you want to raise it, but it isn't directly related to the objective, jot it down on a note and at the end of the meeting I'll look at it."

10 minutes to go, and it's time for a strong finish.

"In summary, we have decided to approve Z. Mo has agreed to complete X today and Amelia has agreed to notify Y of the decision by tomorrow afternoon. Both will confirm with me once they've done it. Next meeting is on June 4th at 11am in this room. Thank you for your participation today."

> **When you are finishing a meeting,**
> **Then confirm the actions arising and the next steps.**

Next time you have a meeting, think of the MEET sandwich. Oh, and don't forget to pick up some bread on your way home.

The bell is for me, not for you!

The school bell is very powerful. It is the symbol of freedom that has the power to instantly transform a willing student into a maniacal football hooligan.

Break times at school are usually pretty short, especially when you have aspirations of necking a bag of crisps and finishing the second half of the 25-a-side football match that started before school.

The conversation on the bus after school is shaped by what happens on that tarmac, and that really matters. With reputations on the line, it isn't just an important thing in their minds - it's **the only** important thing.

The last lesson before break time is like the TV build up to the FA Cup Final. Imaginations run wild and excitement builds. For that pupil, the final countdown starts with 15 minutes of the lesson to go. In the final 5 minutes, in your mind you are walking down that tunnel at a packed Wembley stadium. It's starting to feel real.

5 minutes to go: Slowly open the zip on your bag without making a sound (not easy).

4 minutes to go: Start putting things into the bag, one by one.

3 minutes to go: The pen goes into the bag, (but you're still pretending to write with an air pen).

2 minutes to go: Subtly slide your arms into the jacket on the back of your chair.

1 minute to go: Your spring is completely coiled, waiting for the moment. 'They think it's all over...'

RIIIIIIIING: '...It is now!'. The last couple of books slam into the bag, the zip whizzes round (not so quietly this time) and 30 chairs scrape simultaneously. Game On.

'Get back to your seat!

What on Earth do you think you're doing!?

The bell is for me, not for you!'

You know how you can always remember your favourite teacher at school? I bet it's not the one that repeatedly churned out that phrase!

People are very sensitive to expectations, and when something has clear start and finish times, like a lesson at school, there is an expectation that we will start on time and finish on time.

> **Is it so unreasonable to expect people to keep to time?**

Years later, in business meetings, not much has changed. Granted, it probably isn't a 25-a-side football match that you want to race off to, but you do have things that you want and need to be doing, so when you've been given a finish time, you want that to actually be the time it finishes.

There is nothing worse than when a meeting is due to finish at 12.30, but at 12.29 the Chair asks if there is 'any other business'. You just know that Martin from Accounts is going to chew everyone's ear off for another 25 minutes about parking in unmarked bays or something. Nightmare.

When you're running a meeting, start on time and finish on time. Even if it means starting before everyone is ready, you should do it. Next time, those stragglers will know that the start time is the start time, and nobody likes the shame of walking into something that's already begun.

Here are a couple of useful tips on starting and finishing on time:

> **In addition to a start time, have an 'arrive' time. "Please arrive by 09.55. The meeting will start promptly at 10.00".**

> Request 'Any Other Business' items be submitted prior to the meeting. This gives people the opportunity to raise what they want to, but more importantly it allows you to control what happens. For most things, you'll find you can deal with them away from a formal meeting structure.

> Everything you do sets a precedent for next time.

A major reason for meetings finishing late is when they start late. It's amazing how many people don't mind turning up late to your meeting but will have a face like a smacked backside if you try to keep them late at the end to make up for it. There's a simple solution:

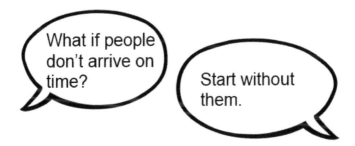

If you're going to set a precedent, make it a good one. Start on time, finish on time. The people who were there on time will appreciate the respect you've shown them, and the people who were late will learn a lesson from it, especially if you make the most valuable part of the meeting the first point on the agenda!

In my experience, when someone gets a reputation for starting and finishing on time, people respect that and respond well to it. Nobody minds an early finish – but everyone hates a late one. Early start, early dart.

Finish
on time

Level Three

Block 10

Strength

The subtle art of dealing with distractions without killing anyone

The door creaks open and a concerned looking head pops round. "Have you got a minute?". It's that dreaded question isn't it... I mean, you have technically 'got' a minute, but you know very well that this will be much more than that.

You can probably relate to this situation, and maybe you can empathise with the struggle it causes many people when they hear it. You've got loads to do already, but when someone you like asks for your help it can be really difficult to turn them down when they come to you.

You feel guilty saying no. You want your clients to be happy and you want to be that person that always makes the time to helps others.

That's lovely, but what you need to remember is that time is finite. Whenever you say yes to something, you are not just saying no to something else by default, but you are saying no to *everything* else. You are essentially making a choice to sacrifice some time that you *could* invest in your health, building relationships or improving your business, and donating it to someone else to invest in those same objectives for themselves. There's nothing wrong with that if it's what you truly want to do, but it's easy to forget the real deal you are making.

So, when you agree to take on someone else's priority, you are sacrificing your own ability to achieve your own goals. I think you know that is not usually a good idea in the grand scheme of things.

Warren Buffet once said, "The difference between successful people and very successful people is that very successful people say no to almost everything". That's because when you break it down, you can either choose to work on your own priority or you can compromise and work on someone else's.

Eleanor Roosevelt said that nobody can make you feel inferior without your permission. In the same vein, nobody can take your time without your permission. You have far more control than you think you do.

Give yourself permission to reject distractions from working on your own priority. In theory I'm sure you agree with that, but you might be wondering how well it works in practice. Let's address that now. Here are a few initial thoughts:

- Start by doing the 20% of things that will take you closest to your own personal goal. The Pareto Principle tells you that you will achieve 80% of your goals if you do that.
- If you're working from home, you'll know that there are a million things flirting with you, all purporting to be more important than what you are doing right now. This is why you need a work bunker. Somewhere you can lock yourself away from others and be free from distractions.
- Do yourself a favour and get your phone and emails serving you instead of ruling you. Your inbox is full of the priorities of other people – remember that.

Let's look at some things that you can use straight away to help you to say No.

The AK-47 approach

Imagine your colleague has far too much to do and is trying to offload a few tasks. Or that a customer is adding demands as favours they're sure you'll help with. Or a peer wants your support in setting something up that could really benefit from your advice...

They select you as their target person, but just as they start to ask you if you will do a particular task for them, they notice you sitting there pointing an AK-47 assault rifle in their direction.

I'm pretty sure they'd get out of your way and avoid doing anything that you might not like, right now!

Of course, I am not advocating that kind of behaviour for a second! I am simply using it as a memorable way for you to master the key elements of a successful 'No':

AK? Assertiveness and Kindness.

If you say no in an assertive and kind way, it really can be just as effective as that assault rifle, so in keeping with the AK-47 theme, here are 47 examples of assertive and kind ways to say 'No':

1. Thanks for the offer but I have way too much on at the moment.

2. Thanks for thinking of me but I can't spare the time at the moment.

3. Ordinarily I'd love to but this week I don't have the time.

4. Sounds great but I already have other plans that I can't change.

5. I'm flattered that you've come to me for help but I can't accommodate anything else at the moment.

6. I really appreciate the vote of confidence but I can't commit to that at the moment.

7. I can empathise with you as I'm really bogged down with things, too.

8. I have so much on this week that I'll have to decline.

9. This week is just chaos for me... I'm sorry I can't help you.

10. I think my head would explode if I tried to take one more thing at the moment! Sorry!

11. I think tonight is going to be a late finish as it is. Sorry!

12. Sorry. If I don't focus on this project I'm going to miss a really

important deadline.

13. I'm working to a tight deadline this week so I can't.

14. I promised I'd get this done today so unfortunately I can't help you.

15. This piece of work is already overdue so I can't think about anything else at the moment.

16. The last thing I want to do is promise something I can't deliver, so I will have to say no.

17. I have too much respect for you to give this anything less than my best, and I can't do that today.

18. This deserves my full attention but I just can't give it that at the moment. Sorry!

19. Sounds like you've got too much on. So have I. Sorry!

20. It seems like you're looking for a quick fix to this and that's not something I can give you at the moment.

21. I don't think I'm your answer to this problem unfortunately as I'm snowed under.

22. I can't fit anything else in today, sorry!

23. You know I would if I could but I really haven't got the capacity to fit this in this week.

24. I can see why you're asking me, but I can't help this time - sorry!

25. I have done this kind of thing before and know it can take more time than I can give it.

26. I know from experience this would take me more time to complete

than I have available this week, so I'll have to decline.

27. If I was to help you I'd want to do it properly, and I don't think I have time to do that now.

28. Giving this less than my best would be unfair on you, and unfortunately I have far too much on my plate at the moment.

29. My time is fully booked with paid clients today.

30. I have back-to-back meetings all afternoon, sorry. Good luck with it!

31. I wish I had time to help you but unfortunately it's allocated elsewhere at the moment.

32. You know I'd always support you if I could, but I am snowed under today.

33. There's a to-do list as long as my arm today. I'll have to say no this time.

34. I've already had to outsource some of my own tasks this week. Sorry!

35. If you find someone with a lot of free time send them my way as I've got a ton of things that need doing, too!

36. My schedule is completely full today, sorry.

37. I've had to postpone meetings today because I'm double-booked.

38. An unexpected problem this morning has left me playing catch-up, so I'm sorry I have no time today.

39. I had to come in early today to keep up with my own stuff so can't take on any more work, but good luck!

40. I'm fixing something urgent for a client today that I can't avoid.

41. There is somewhere I need to be all afternoon, sorry!

42. I have something I really need to get finished today so I'll have to say no this time.

43. That's a great idea but I don't have time.

44. I like your thinking but I'm not able to help with it right now.

45. With more notice I might have been able to but I'm sorry I can't do anything to help right now.

46. This sounds like it deserves more time than I can give to it at the moment. Sorry.

47. That's the kind of project I'd love to give my full attention to, which I can't today.

I hope there is enough ammunition in the above list to arm you for the next time you need to defend your time. Yes, some of them may seem obvious, but they're usually the opportunities we miss. And if some seem repetitive, then maybe get into that habit of repeating them, because they obviously hold weight!

Oh, and remember, you're not obliged to apologise.

An unlikely business guru's top tip

Saying no is a skill, and thankfully there are plenty of business gurus to learn from. You've probably heard of Zig Ziglar and Brian Tracy, but here's a name you probably didn't expect... Vicky Pollard.

VICKY POLLARD? The gobby teenager from the BBC comedy, Little Britain?

Yep. That's her.

When Vicky, played by Matt Lucas (yes, a large part of the comedy lies in the fact that it's a grown man playing the role of a teenage girl), is asked to do something she doesn't want to do, she says, "Yeah but, no but, yeah but, no but...". You can learn from that, believe it or not.

When you are asked to help with something when you don't have the time or the desire to do so, you could say:

"Yes, but can you do this for me?"

"Yes, but it will cost ..."

"Yes, but not before Wednesday."

or

"No, but I suggest you do this"

"No, but if I were you I'd speak to..."

"No, but if anything changes I'll let you know"

You might like these suggestions, or you might not. The words you use should be your own, but either way I can guarantee that you won't magically come up with the right words and deliver them perfectly if you wing it.

Most people don't rise to new heights in the face of a challenge. They usually sink to the level of their preparation, so it is advisable to practice the situation many times so that you are ready for it the next time it happens.

It is often said that practice makes perfect. It doesn't. Practice makes *permanent*, so make sure that you make your rehearsals as realistic as possible.

Select your preferred statement and say it aloud, confidently in front of the mirror. Get eye-contact with yourself and be as natural as you can. If you do this 50 times, I guarantee you'll feel better about saying it. Do it 100 times and I'd be surprised if it doesn't feel quite natural to say.

Remember that after you've made your response, hold the silence. This shows that you're committed to what you've said, and doesn't allow for you to end up talking yourself back into something you really don't have time to do!

Just try not to say or do anything else like Vicky Pollard... It probably won't be well received!

When things distract you

With the best will in the world, things will distract you during the day. We've just spent some time considering how we can deal with colleagues, but there are millions of other potential distractions around you as well. If you work from home, there will always be things that *need* to be done in the house – you can't escape it.

My advice in dealing with distractions is really just a case of making some things easier and some things more difficult.

For example, you can make it *easier* to get into 'the zone' by creating a specific environment for yourself; in a quiet place, with your headphones in, and your timer set for an hour.

You can also make it more *difficult* for things to distract you by changing the notification settings on your phone, and communicating clearly with people around you that you need to be left undisturbed.

This works whether you are working in a busy office or on your own from home. When something distracts you, make a note of it and then do something (anything you can) to make it either easier for you to ignore it or more difficult for it to distract you again.

Plan logically, not emotionally

Have you ever watched an FA Cup football match? Both teams enter the match with carefully selected line-ups, a logical strategy based on form, and a tactical masterplan of how to overcome the opposition with style and grace. Early in the game, the passing is a joy to watch and the teams seem to play in a patient and deliberate way that will be broken only by the flair of the opposition doing something daring, impressive... or lucky.

But then, as the minutes play on towards the dreaded suggestion of penalties, where one team shows they so desperately need a goal more than the opposition, the whole gracefully logical plan seems to get kicked right out of the equation. All of a sudden, the team chasing the game completely changes their approach, and starts to desperately, impatiently and almost emotionally launch the ball aggressively forwards at every opportunity. It's an attitude of 'eventually this has to pay off!' Well, if they thought that this was the best way to ever score, why didn't they just adopt that tactic from the start?

It seems like a classic case of planning and making decisions based on emotion in place of logic. We all do it sometimes, especially when time is running out, there's a deadline, and we need to get something done. Before you know it, your deliberately constructed plan of short work sprints to allow you to be more productive is replaced with a desperate flurry of frustration and anger as you work for hours without a break to 'get it done'.

Just like the 'long ball' approach in our analogy, this doesn't usually work. Stick to what you know is the most effective approach and trust the process. Plan and make decisions with logic – not emotion.

Level Three

Block 11

Balance

Achieve PROPER balance in your life

Is your life like a wonky table?

Imagine your life is a table, with all your goals and all the things you want to achieve sitting on top of it.

The table has 4 legs (as you would expect), but one or more of the legs are wobbly or a different length... generally making the whole thing a little unbalanced. Everything on the top is now unstable.

The four legs can broadly represent different areas of your life:

- Physical health
- Mental health
- Work
- Relationships

Quite often, people neglect (consciously or subconsciously) one or more of these aspects in life in favour of giving more attention to others. For example, they may be doing really well at work... but not exercising or eating well enough, not putting enough into their relationships, and feeling stressed out and alone in the process.

Or, maybe they play too hard and their work suffers.

You can often identify a wonky leg when you talk to people.

The amount of time and attention each of the legs needs varies from person to person, but it's important to understand your own life and find the right balance for your 'table'. The happiest people I know have the best balance. PROPER balance. The mix between your PROfessional life, and your PERsonal life.

Do you have PROPER balance?

Achieve
PRO|PER
life balance

Quality time

When you think of spending quality time with your family, what springs to mind?

For millions of people, their version of quality time is sitting in front of the television with their partner, simultaneously scrolling through social media on their smart phones.

It's a habit that these people probably do automatically. One that, if they thought about it, they would undoubtedly agree that it is not quality time at all.

Equally misunderstood is the concept of quality time with children. Multiple studies have shown that a large portion of parent-child interaction consists of giving instructions/warnings, and arguing about things like eating veg, going to bed at a certain time, and not kicking seven shades out of siblings at any point in the process.

Even with this included, the average parent is believed to spend less than half an hour per day directly communicating with their children.

I'm sure you'll agree that this is not quality family time. So what can you do about it?

Here are some suggestions that you can implement immediately to get more quality in your quality time:

If you like watching TV there's no reason to cut it completely out, but why not limit it to a certain time frame, and instead spend time looking at family photos, talking about your dreams and ambitions (not arguing about work), sharing funny stories, cooking together, going for a walk.

Connecting with our kids is a critically endangered act in the busy world we live in. Insist on having some quality time every day, such as an evening meal sitting at the table together with no tech (yes, this is possible!) Even if your children eat earlier than you, you can still sit with them.

Avoid one-word answers in any interactions you have by asking open questions that start fun discussions, descriptions and recounts.

You can also get quality time for your health, too. I challenge you to do one of these things every day for 2 weeks and not feel both mentally and physically better for it:

- Go for a 30-minute walk at lunchtime every day
- Start a run-streak and commit to running a minimum of one mile per day
- Switch off all technology and read a book for the last 30 minutes of your day before bed
- Go to bed just half an hour earlier than you normally do
- Get up half an hour earlier than usual and have some quiet time to yourself before you start your day.

Each of these things would only take half an hour (that you could probably cut from your TV or phone time) to achieve but would make a massive difference to your life in the process.

Sounds like an effective use of time, doesn't it? Why wouldn't you do it? Probably because whilst it is easy to do, it is also easy *not* to do! That's why it's a good idea to work together on it with someone who can hold you accountable (and vice versa).

Level Three

Block 12

Habits

Time habits

As mentioned much earlier in the book, a Google search of 'Time Management' produces over four and a half billion results, yet most people still struggle to manage their time. We are literally drowning in information - but starving for a little bit of wisdom.

It's infuriating, isn't it, when you know what you should be doing but you just don't do it. It happens in life all the time.

- With your diet

- With your exercise routine

- When you need to make **that** phone call

Digging deeper into those Google results, many of the tips you'll find will point to decisions, choices and priorities as the answers to effective time management. Whilst I agree these are important considerations, they don't tell the full story, and here's why:

> **Around half of what you do on a day-to-day basis is not a conscious choice. It's habitual.**

A great deal of what you do every day is beyond the immediate control of your priorities and the choices you make. It's about your habits and the things you do routinely.

The lightbulb moment in my own personal journey with Time Mastery was when I started to notice the habits I had. I was doing many of the same things, in the same way, at the same time, every single day.

For months, I'd been trying every Time Management strategy I could get my hands on. Some of them worked and some of them didn't, and I wanted to understand why. I came to realise that I spend large portions of my day on autopilot, following my routine:

- Wake up at around 6.50am, and wait for my 7am alarm

- The same bathroom routine

- Walk the same route with the dog

- Get the kettle on and toast some bread

...and that is before I even start my working day, which I started to notice followed another set of routines.

I'll bet that any time strategies that currently work for you are the ones that most easily managed to settle themselves into your routine.

**If you make effective Time Management into a habit,
it becomes way more 'sticky'**

Textbooks from the last few decades will show that the common belief was that it took 21 days to form a habit. Then people started to suggest it was more like 66 days. I read somewhere more recently that it takes between 18 and 254 days. Brilliant. The reality is that you need to keep doing something until YOU personally start to do it automatically as part of your routine. Everyone is different, and some habits take longer to form than others.

New habits can be formed much more easily when they use an existing habit to get them up to speed. I use a specific approach, called 'When and Then' to help me attach desired actions to existing habits. You will see examples of this being used throughout this book already.

Just like you hopefully already have habits such as '*When* I go to the toilet, *Then* I wash my hands', you can use one action as the cue for another desirable action. For example, I knew I should pick up the phone more, instead of hiding behind emails and text messages, but it was a habit for me to just get typing, and it can be hard to break habits. I needed a new trigger to make me pick up the phone, so I changed my auto-signature on my email so that it read, "Should this be a phone call?"

So now, clicking 'Compose New Email' brings up a trigger question for me to consider whether or not it would save me time to get a quick answer over the phone rather than type an email, wait for a response, then probably have to type another response after that.

Often, it is better to give someone a call, and if it isn't, it only takes a second to delete the line and continue typing the email.

Here are 5 'When and Then' examples that can be used as triggers to help you to develop time habits:

1. When you have an idea, *Then* capture it in your phone notes for later.

2. When you need to focus, *Then* go off-site and offline.

3. When you feel overwhelmed, *Then* write everything down and categorise the list.

4. When you're invited to a group meeting, *Then* ask for the agenda to check you can contribute before accepting or respectfully declining.

5. When you write an email, *Then* check it for CSI.

Let me explain that last one...

When it comes to Time Thieves, email is a key crime scene for us to investigate. Whilst CSI would usually be an acronym for Crime Scene Investigation, in this instance it's a memorable checklist to help you to get quicker replies to your emails (it also works for voicemails, too).

C – Clear. Is it clear enough what you are actually asking for in the email?

S – Short. Nobody wants to write - or read - an overly long email. Keep it short.

I – Interesting. Go through your message from the receiver's perspective. Does it make you want to jump into action - or jump into bed for a snooze?

> **When you have written an email and are about to hit send,**
> **Then check it for CSI.**

Your time habits shape the quality of your life as well as your time. If you want to **do** better, you need to consistently **be** better. It's about time.

Streaking is fun

I've had some crazy ideas in my time, but the one that really made people think I'd lost the plot was when I said I was going to prepare for the London Marathon by streaking.

After a few awkward moments of confusion, I explained myself. I'm not sure if people actually thought my plan was a good one, or if they were just relieved that I wasn't going to start running up and down the street in my birthday suit.

> **To clarify, you can keep your clothes on.**
> **In fact, I'd encourage it.**

Streaking is a really effective tool in the early stages of developing a new habit. It essentially consists of doing a particular action for as many consecutive days as possible without breaking the chain.

One of the main reasons streaking works so well is simple. The more consecutive days you achieve, the more you'd have to lose by missing a day – and the annoyance of being 'beaten' is a killer. Believe me, there were some cold and rainy days in my run streak that might have persuaded me to have a day off, had it not been for my streak. No matter how wet and cold it was, I was always pleased that I'd been out for that run when I got back. The hardest bit was always getting started, and so it was very rare that I stopped at the minimum required distance of a mile. I'd get into my stride and carry on for at least a few miles most days.

It sounds obvious but it feels really good to achieve something, however small. There is nothing more motivational than progress, and the principle of streaking takes advantage of that.

Having signed up to my first London Marathon in 2011, I downloaded a specific 16-week training plan. My first thought was one of overwhelm. Maybe I shouldn't have been surprised that preparations for a marathon would include a hell of a lot of running, but it looked like a big challenge to say the least.

Before getting into it, I felt I needed to get used to running every day, so I told everyone who would listen that I committed to running at least one mile every day for a month, and that I would post the GPS proof of it online every day to hold myself accountable. I was trying to build a little bit of pressure so that I would look daft if I didn't achieve it, and it worked. My run streak finally ended the day after I'd completed the Marathon. Mission complete (plus I could barely run a bath on that day, let alone a mile).

In a business, setting the principle is just the same. Whether it's committing to:

- 5 sales calls every morning

- 30 minutes of content creation

- A short walk to give you the time and space to get your thoughts together...

> **If something would be beneficial to do every day you can use streaking to make it a habit**

Sounds easy doesn't it? Don't be fooled, though. Complacency can lead you to make the mistake of trying to do a few of these new things every day, but it is usually best to **focus on just one thing at a time.** The most valuable one to you at that point.

Assessing 'The Domino Effect' will help you make this choice – and I don't mean go and order a pizza.

Have you ever seen the crazy chain reaction videos on the internet? They start with something really simple like a marble rolling into a release catch for a pulley system...

Which flies up and knocks a bigger ball down another tube and onto the button of a kettle...

Which boils and creates steam to make a balloon rise into nudging a toy car onto a track...

Which follows a track and loop-the-loops before doing all sorts of other crazy things.

It's really good to see The Domino Effect of one object going through the action of 'knocking on' to the next.

Habits work in a similar way. Every action has a reaction, and there is a natural domino effect that can be experienced If you start with one simple thing that can lead to another.

For example, 'scheduling time to schedule your time' creates a domino effect. What gets scheduled gets done, so you'll sit down and plan out a structure for what you're going to do and when you're going to do it. In doing this, the next domino falls and you start to anticipate problems such as travel times, so you move things around and confirm them, and make your days flow a lot more efficiently. This leads to something else, and so on.

So that's why The Domino Effect is so important. It's the positive time habit that will trigger a lot of other positive actions automatically. Focus on that one first.

> **The first domino creates a chain reaction.**
> **Choose it wisely!**

> **When you want to improve something,**
> **Then select 'the domino' to push.**

The streak accelerator

We have already established that it is difficult to predict how long it will take to form a new habit, and that doing the desired action repeatedly for as long as it takes for it to become a habit for you personally is the way to achieve it.

There is, however, a way to accelerate this process. It's most commonly used in elite sports.

When it comes to practice, the brain struggles to distinguish between thoughts and reality, and athletes take advantage of that through visualisation and mental rehearsal.

Golfers mentally rehearse their pre-swing process to put themselves into the right frame of mind for a successful putt. Footballers imagine taking that free kick and seeing it fly into the top corner. Sprinters experience themselves reacting to the gun and making a great start.

In many cases, visualisation is actually more effective than physical practice, because not only can you get unlimited repetition without physical strain, but under the right conditions you can also replicate the pressures and environmental factors you'd experience on the big day.

Visualisation is a key part of sport science and there's a strong case for it to be used a lot more in business, too.

You can visualise yourself acting exactly how you would like to in difficult conversations. A great mentor of mine, Andy Bounds, suggests practicing difficult conversations - and it really works. When you are comfortable with what you'll say and how you'll say it, you come across more confidently and get better results. Equally, he suggests practicing the first sentence of a big presentation hundreds of times, because it sets the tone for the rest of it.

Practice makes things permanent, and the untapped opportunity of being able to practice things way more is something you should consider if you want to accelerate your habit-forming ability.

Practice

Think of an occasion in business that you dread, and commit to practicing it/visualising the scenario at least 10 times every day. Select the most appropriate time and schedule it in as a part of your daily routine. Here are some examples of what you might like to practice:

- The moment when people say your prices are too high
- The first sentence of the presentation you are due to deliver
- The 'Right First Time' morning approach
- Your favourite way to say 'No'
- How to stop a conversation veering off track in a meeting

If you can anticipate uncomfortable situations, you can mentally prepare for them.

Rewards

Rewards reinforce behaviour. I'm sure you probably already know that, but do you use them to reinforce your *own* behaviours when you try/do/complete what you need to do?

Rewards don't have to be a huge wad of cash (as much as that is lovely to receive)! In fact, there are loads of really effective rewards that you can use that don't cost much, if anything at all. Here are some examples:

1. **Congratulate yourself** - It may sound strange, but this is actually an effective way of making yourself feel good about what you've just done.

2. **Put a big tick on today's calendar** - Using visual markers can help you to remember how far you've come and encourage you to keep going.

3. **Take a look at your written vision** - Imagine yourself one step closer to achieving it.

4. **Give yourself a break** - Allow yourself 5 minutes to make a brew and relax. Take a deep breath and bask in your own glory for a moment!

5. **Tell someone** - Share your good news with someone who will be happy for you - or the person holding you accountable (who will also hopefully be very happy for you). Their encouragement will feel great!

6. **Post on social media** - If social networking is your thing, you will enjoy the encouragement and engagement that comes from sharing positive news. Just don't spend the rest of the day

checking for replies!

7. **Listen to your favourite song** - Associate things you enjoy with achieving your daily goals.

8. **Go to bed early or have a lie in** – You'll enjoy it in the short term and benefit in the long term!

9. **Have a relaxing bath** – Maybe even light some candles!

10. **Get outside for a bit of fresh air** – Even walking around the block can give you a change of scenery and a chance to reflect on the good job you've done. Call it a victory lap!

11. **Read the latest updates on your favourite team** – Or anything you like to be honest. Just keep it positive, which usually means avoiding the news!

12. **Leave someone a voice message** – If you haven't spoken to someone you care about for a while, leaving them a voice message can make them happy, and make you feel good as a result. Hopefully they'll respond later in the day and give you something to look forward to. Plus – it's quicker and more personal than writing a text!

Whether you like one of the ideas above or prefer one of your own, it is a good idea to reward yourself for achieving your goals. It will encourage you to do more of the same in the future!

Seven time habits of highly efficient people:

Put simply, the efficiency of something is the amount of output it generates in relation to the energy it uses up in the process. Just like energy efficient boilers use less energy to kick out more heat, the most efficient people can generate results quicker than the average Joe.

When you look closely at the most efficient people in your life, what similarities do you see between them? Here are my top seven observations from watching highly efficient people in action.

1. They are brilliant learners

No matter how efficient you get, you can always get a little bit better. The most efficient people know this and are always looking for marginal improvements, like a Formula One racing team would always be trying to shave another hundredth of a second off a lap time. They know that every little improvement adds up to a big difference over time.

If you want to be a better learner, why not dedicate an hour a day to reading – perhaps taking it out of the time you'd usually spend watching TV? It's estimated that if you did this every day on the topic of your choice, within just a few years you would rank in the top 1% of people globally for knowledge in that subject.

Imagine what that could mean for you!

Now that might seem a little bit far fetched for you, but it isn't an all or nothing deal. Every day you do it you are improving yourself just a little bit more. So why not start a reading streak? Even reading just one page per day would be a good start and will help you to start developing daily reading (and learning) into a habit.

If you don't have the time or inclination to read, listen to more audiobooks. It's the same principle. Just start with a little bit each day and go from there. If you select a topic that you enjoy and an appropriate time to do it, you should find it fairly easy to build a substantial streak. For me, walking the dog is a perfect opportunity to put my headphones in and listen to a few chapters.

It is such an incredible opportunity to be able to benefit from a lifetime of experience, condensed into a few hundred pages or a few hours of audio. By not only learning from your own mistakes but those of others as well, you are accelerating your own personal development in exceptional efficiency.

Imagine what an effect it would have on your business if you committed to learning something every day that can have a positive effect on your business and your life.

Nelson Mandela once famously said, "Education is the most powerful weapon which you can use to change the world". I'm not saying you have to change the world, but if you can change *your* world for the better, you definitely should.

2. They plan ahead

Abraham Lincoln had it right when he famously said, "Give me six hours to chop down a tree and I will spend the first four sharpening the axe". Our tools and preparation are everything. Some of the most efficient people I know swear by putting pen to paper on a Sunday afternoon to plan out the week ahead.

Of course, these people don't pack out all of their time. Far from it. They simply schedule the most important drivers of their success to make sure they are afforded the time they require to be achieved, and then they stick to it. It's as simple as that. If you don't ringfence the time then other things will encroach into it, leaving you with less time than is required to do the things that will in turn achieve your goals.

Remember to include financial projections and cash flow forecasts in your plans. If you need help with this, you can ask your accountant – they'll more than likely be very happy to see you planning in this way!

3. They automate tasks

There are plenty of affordable online apps that can automate almost any admin-based process for you. This is especially the case for finance-based tasks, such as invoicing. It's very common for small businesses to get slack on invoicing. They'll send out invoices late, which means they get paid late, and that puts unnecessary strain on cash flow, which then puts strain on you as the business owner. When it is implemented correctly, automation is the epitome of efficiency. It'll send out your invoices on time - every time. It'll send reminders if necessary (depending on your payment terms) and reconcile your accounts when the payment is received.

This is just one example (of many) of how efficient people use automation in their business. The possibilities are endless, from marketing to sales, and emailing to customer service. Make it a habit to consider whether the things you are doing repeatedly could be automated.

4. They have a great business model

A fantastic accountant I know advocates that if the business model is broken, you'll be forever going round in circles (getting stressed, losing time, etc), regardless of your turnover.

When developing new courses, services or products, efficient people don't make the mistake of spending hours and hours getting it absolutely perfect, only to release it and realise it had all been a waste of time. No way! They pre-sell, very often before doing any of the work towards it at all, because they know that if there's no demand for it, it isn't going to be worth doing! Once they have established the demand is there, they'll create prototypes for parts of it, test them, improve them, and then add to them until they're right. Then they release it, knowing it works and having already sold a load of them in advance.

Remember, turnover is vanity, profit is sanity. Don't obsess over turnover alone. I know plenty of 'six-figure' businesses run by directors who take home little more than minimum wage. Equally I know plenty of businesses who have a pretty modest turnover but a very enviable nett profit margin.

Assessing all areas of your business model on a regular basis is a good habit to get into. This is one of the many reasons working with a coach can be a good idea for business owners, as they can provide an informed, objective perspective.

5. They communicate really well

I always maintain that the most successful, happy and well-adjusted business owners I ever see have 3 things in common that they all do well.

- They have clarity

- They are consistent

- They communicate really effectively

In practice, an easy thing to do to ensure great communication is simply to ask more questions. Ask exactly what is expected and it can save you doing pages of work when a paragraph would have sufficed.

Ask what the desired outcomes are for a meeting.

Ask what the goals are for the team for the day.

For tight deadlines you're worried about, ask colleagues for help, or if you're really struggling, request a deadline extension. Either way, the earlier you ask the better.

When it comes to the sales process (and a lot of other processes too, for that matter), the main reason people don't get the sale is because they don't ask for it.

Commit to asking more questions, and start an asking streak. Maybe one a day, maybe 10 a day. Find what works for you, and know that if you ask at least 365 extra questions this year, you should certainly be able to enjoy some more yesses!

An ask a day keeps the maybes away.

6. They run a tight ship when it comes to their finances

It is a well-known fact that cash flow is one of the biggest killers of small businesses. Many a profitable business has gone under because although they are owed a lot of money, they don't have enough in the bank account to survive until those invoices clear.

Accounting can be one of those tasks for a business owner that gets delayed, probably because there often isn't anyone pushing you to do it (and you don't really want to do any of the tasks associated with it, either).

You can make better decisions if they are based on up-to-date information, yet so many businesses submit their accounts a few months after the year end and are only ever reviewing out-of-date information. Programmes like Xero allow you to automate parts of the process, giving you live, useful info for information-based decision making.

If you want to make better decisions for your business today whilst ensuring you'll be around for a long time to come, you need to stay on top of your accounting. Whether you do it yourself or enlist the help of a professional, it's an unavoidable time habit to adopt if you want that thriving business we have been talking about in this book.

Instead of trying to do it all at once, why not break it down into little chunks and get into the habit of doing a little bit every week? You'll be able to review costs, monitor cash, and make projections for the future.

7. They respect their own time

Try and get a meeting with a truly efficient and successful person and I'd be very surprised if they just open their door to you without setting any boundaries. In many ways, they protect their time as vehemently as a goose fiercely protecting its young. Stay within the acceptable limits and everything will be fine, but don't take liberties.

The most efficient people I know make it clear to you from the outset how much time they have, and aim to be as generous as they can in their time rather than with their time. That's the important decision, and a Time Habit that can make you way more efficient.

Level Four

Block 13

Autonomy

You're the boss

Autonomy means deciding what you do, how you do it, and when you do it.

For many people, autonomy over their own time is a key reason for them choosing self-employment over working for someone else. The problem is that there is a misconception with self-employment that you can take time off whenever you like, but there are so many reasons why this is rarely the case.

A common feeling of people who work on their own is that they give themselves a hard time about not working. They force themselves to work long hours for low pay doing all sorts of jobs within the business that they don't really want to do. It's almost as if they have made themselves into the worst boss ever and then employed themselves! They feel as though if they don't throw absolutely everything into their business, it's never going to be successful.

Under promise and over deliver

It's a similar story when it comes to dealing with clients. I have lost count of the number of people I have spoken to as a coach who agree to client onboarding or deadlines that they know they shouldn't, and end up stressing themselves out. They only want to please their clients, so it comes from a good place, but in reality they end up leaving less time for health and family, and totally stress themselves out.

Ironically this makes them less effective and results in work that is less than their best, often missing the deadlines they promised in the first place. They quickly realise the irony of promising the earth to clients to make them happy, but then making them unhappy by failing to deliver on the promise.

Delay your promises

If you are the kind of person who gets excited by a project and are at risk of agreeing to deadlines you will struggle to meet, you need to develop a helpful Time Habit to minimise the potential damage.

> **When you are asked to commit to a deadline for a project or a time for a meeting,**
> **Then you should delay your promise.**

I'd always advocate saying something like, "If I promise something to you I want to be sure I can deliver it, so if it's OK I will check my diary when I'm back in the office and confirm it with you this evening". There aren't many people who will have a problem with that. Imagine them saying "No, we want you to commit now and then potentially let us down, please". It isn't going to happen.

That delay will enable you to carefully consider your schedule and only make promises that you can stick to once you've given everything more thought.

Develop your self confidence

Confidence is a funny thing, isn't it? It seems to be in a constant state of change; either growing or shrinking depending on your most recent experiences. You can find yourself in a cycle quite easily, and this can be positive or negative.

For example, if you've just given a presentation and it went really well, your confidence in presenting will grow. This will make you more likely to present well next time, and lead to even more confidence in the future.

Equally, if something doesn't go well, your confidence can be damaged, and this makes you less likely to do a good job of it next time. It's easy to get into cycles.

By understanding this, you can take control of your confidence by giving yourself 'small wins'. If your confidence is hit by something, do something you know you're good at to stop a negative cycle before it builds momentum. By experiencing some success as soon as possible, you can take back ownership of your confidence, and that can be an important step in gaining autonomy over your time.

Remember why you are doing this

Whether you're in employment or you're self-employed, it is important that you give yourself permission to spend time on the things that will bring you happiness. True autonomy allows you to focus on the most important things - in and out of work - and create an environment where everything else is done around you. As outlined in the 'Balance' block of the pyramid, the four legs of your table must be balanced or the whole thing will become unstable.

Sacrificing relationships and health to fit in work deadlines is seldom a wise move. It would be like sacrificing air to have more food and water. You need them all, and you need enough of each of them. That's balance, and you shouldn't ever feel bad about having it.

You started this process by setting the foundations of your pyramid, including your Why and your Vision.

The number of people who are choosing to construct their work around their lives rather than look for the job that gives security, a bumper pay packet, and a fixed schedule, is seriously on the up.

In reality, permission is only half the battle. You need to have the tools and habits in place to help you succeed, and by the time you reach this point in the pyramid, you should have plenty of those in place.

Level Four

Block 14

Influence

Your A-Team

"If you have a problem, if no one else can help, and if you can find them, maybe you can hire the A-Team."

If you know that line, you'll probably recall The A-Team from the 1980s, or at least the remake movie in 2010. It's a term often used to describe a group of people who are absolutely brilliant at what they do.

> **If you could have an A-Team of people around you,
> who would you want to be in it?**

They say you're the average of the people you spend the most time with. Your mood, your thinking and a large chunk of your behaviour is all influenced by your environment and those people within it.

If you imagine your ambitions and potential as a flame, some people will be fanning those flames and helping them to grow, and others will be pouring sand on them. In different contexts, you probably need both of those people at different moments in time. You need to be pushed and encouraged to drive forwards, but equally you sometimes need to know when to slow down a bit.

The A-Team (in terms of the TV show/film) basically consisted of a leader (Hannibal), a smooth talker (Face), a tough guy (BA Baracus), and a highly-skilled specialist (Murdock, the pilot). They were all very different in terms of personality and behaviour traits, but ultimately had complementary skills that brought out the best in one another.

Whether or not you agree with the theory that you are the average of the people you spend the most time with doesn't matter too much, but I'm pretty sure you will agree that your surroundings can have an effect on your behaviour and performance.

Imagine the different behaviours of someone in three different environments:

- In a sales meeting at work with a prospect that could be a massive customer

- At a rock concert with old school friends

- Playing with their children at home

The same person can behave in very different ways when influenced by different environments.

Behaviour and performance are greatly affected by environment.

It may not seem obvious at first, but you have way more control than you think about the people you spend most of your time with. OK, so you can't really choose your family, and maybe you can't always decide who you will need to work with on different tasks, but there is another way that you can spend more time with people.

It is important that you surround yourself with people who have a positive influence on you. You will know some of these people in real-life, but there is an unlimited number of other influences you can access, too. Even people on TV or characters in books... they all count if you're spending a lot of time with them. Similarly, if you follow certain figures online, they count, too. Whoever they are, there's a good chance you'll be able to track down even more of them in books, videos and a multitude of other ways with a simple Google search.

Can they form part of your A-Team? Of course! Your A-Team is made up of the people who you choose to surround yourself with and spend time with to influence you to move closer to your goals. It doesn't matter how they do that – or if they're even real.

Interestingly, the brain struggles to distinguish between what it sees in real life and what it watches on video. That's why you can feel like you really know and 'get' your favourite celebrity even though you've never met them, or why you feel heartbroken when a fictional character dies in a TV show or movie that you like. It's crazy really, isn't it? It works, though.

You can choose anyone to be part of your A-Team, no matter if you've never met them, or if they are still alive (or were ever even real in the first place). The beauty of written and digital content is that it's immortal. Long after a person has died, people can still take inspiration from their words of wisdom.

A word of caution: As easy as it is to find positive influences online, it is even easier to find negative ones. Social media in particular is rife with arrogance, self-importance and negativity. I'm not saying you shouldn't use social media - I think it's great - but the key is to be deliberate with the influences you surround yourself with. If you're searching for inspiration, make sure you're driving the search and not being a passenger in it.

Who's in your A-Team? Write it down and make a conscious effort to surround yourself with them as often as possible.

Be careful who you spend time with

①27andahalf*
WAYS TO IMPROVE YOUR BUSINESS

The A-Team:

1. _____

2. _____

3. _____

4. _____

5. _____

> **When** you want inspiration,
>
> **Then** turn to your A-Team.

It's ok to have plenty of people in your life who aren't in your A-Team. I mean, we can't choose our family and we often can't choose our colleagues, so in being surrounded by those people a lot, we need to be deliberate about the impact we let them have on our lives.

How to keep friends and influence people (to respect your time)

It's all very well managing your *own* time, but there are a lot of things that *other people* do that have a big effect on our time. Here are a few things you can do to influence clients and colleagues to respect your time:

- **Charge up front**: When you've paid for something you get more serious about it. People will value your time more if they have paid for it, so consider getting a financial commitment from them in advance. If nothing else, it will save you from ever having to chase invoices.
- **Don't answer the phone**: Faced with the choice of probably being able to sort something yourself or calling someone and letting them sort it for you, a lot of people will go for the latter option. As a result, you will get people calling you with problems that they could probably solve themselves. By choosing not to answer the call and returning it an hour or so later, you urge them to solve their problem themselves. Text them back in an hour and they'll often thank you for returning their message and then explain that they've already managed to solve the problem.
- **Delay before replying:** If you get an instant message or email and you reply straight away, you are often met with another instant message and find yourself in a conversation where the other person now expects instantaneous responses. Remember, everything you do sets a precedent, both to yourself and others, so the more you respond instantly, the more it will be expected.
- **Make the next move yours**: When you speak to a potential client, make sure that you don't leave without clarifying the next step. Doing this will eliminate those horrible feelings of whether you should chase them. Will they think you're desperate? Will they think you're not really bothered? Nobody wants those feelings, so do yourself a favour and avoid them!

- **Bait the hook**: If you leave uninspiring emails or voice messages for people you cannot be surprised when they don't rush to respond to you. Keep is short, and don't give them all of the answers they want in your message, otherwise they have no reason to call you back. Get into the habit of leaving out a key part out of your message that they'll need to call you for, and you'll encourage them to call you back a lot quicker. Think about it like this – if the Doctor called and left a message to say he/she had your results back, you'd call back quickly, wouldn't you? Obviously, this only applies if you want and need the person to call you back at all!

- **Be clear about what you do**: The number one question you will ever be asked about your business is, 'What do you do?'. How well do you answer that question? It can be the difference between someone wanting to find out more – and someone wanting to find a way out of the conversation.

- **Talk in terms of the other person's interests**: Someone asked me recently how they could bypass the 'current situation' small talk at the beginning of every conversation. My answer was to say what you want to say, but in terms of the other person's interests. So, you could start a conversation with, "I bet you are sick of talking about X all the time, so I'll get straight to the point". That solved the problem instantly.

- **Listen and learn:** If you look at customer reviews of services in your sector (your own and your competitors), you can pick up key phrases that are repeated about what they like and don't like. If you use those phrases when you promote your product you can easily build a connection with your customers, who will feel as though you really understand them.

- **Teach:** If you hear something new it may stick with you for a little while. If you apply that wisdom or lesson to your life, then the learning will become more meaningful. And, if you teach it to someone else... it will fully sink in. Teaching someone else about what you've learned about Time Mastery has the double benefit of influencing others and reinforcing your own learning.

- **Insist on an agenda:** If the desired outcomes of a meeting are not clear, don't waste your time on it. If you are arranging the meeting an agenda will make it clear what you want to achieve and therefore more likely to achieve it. If it's someone else's meeting, ask them for the agenda so you can check whether or not you will be able to contribute to any of it.

- **Under promise, over deliver:** If you think you can do something by Tuesday, promise it by the end of Wednesday. Then, if it takes longer than expected and you deliver it on Wednesday, you'll have held your promise, and if you get it to them a day early on Tuesday, they'll be delighted. An example of the complete opposite of this is my washing machine. It tells me on its digital screen that there are 5 minutes left on a spin, so I come back in 5 minutes and it tells me there are 7 minutes left! It's infuriating! Does yours do that or is mine broken...?

- **Respect your own time:** How can you expect people to respect your time if you don't respect it yourself? At the start of the meeting make it clear when you need it to finish, and stick to it. It can feel rude to cut a meeting short, but if you've agreed the finish time from the start, nobody can have an issue with it.

- **Respect other people's time**: Of course, the rule of reciprocity means that people will often mirror your actions. It's the same principle as when someone sends you a Christmas card and you feel the need to send one back. If you respect people's time, they will respect yours in return. It's here where you can lead by example. If you demand good timekeeping, demonstrate it yourself. If you tell someone you'll meet them at 9am, turn up at 8.50. If the office closes at 6pm, you should encourage everyone to stick to that.

- **Speak last:** The great Nelson Mandela used to always speak last in any meetings he led. It is pretty common for the person leading a meeting to do the majority of the talking at the beginning, before asking the opinion of the other attendees and then summarising at the end. Apparently, Mandela would let everyone have their say and get their thoughts and feelings out in a way that is not biased by his initial thoughts. This would enable him to take time considering multiple perspectives and opinions before summarising the discussion in an informed way. Imagine how that made the people in his meetings feel! I expect if you were called to a meeting with the great Nelson Mandela, and you knew you'd be asked to contribute in such a way, you would not only feel 10 feet tall, but you'd also make sure you were more prepared than ever before for that meeting! That kind of leadership isn't accidental. It's inspirational, and it is undoubtedly a tremendous use of time and respect.

Remember, the leader sets the environment, and the environment sets the behaviour.

I'll give you 10 minutes

It's true, I'm a geek. When I am inspired by someone, I like to contact them to learn even more about them - if they'll allow it, of course. In doing this, I have spotted a common theme. They always respect their own time to such a level that it makes you respect it, too.

I once emailed someone I really respected in business to see if they would give me some advice. I'd read their book and wanted to talk to them. I'm glad I did, and not just because of what they said but also how they said it. It was a perfect example of respecting their own time. They said, "Email my PA and tell them I've asked you to request a 10-minute call with me". That was step one and two in setting the expectation all at once – 1. They have a PA so they must be busy, and 2. If it's a 10-minute call I'll have to get straight to the point. So, I booked, and when the day came I waited for their call at the agreed time. Just as the second hand clicked over, the phone rang at the exact minute they promised. That was point number 3. When they say something, they mean it! I got straight to the point on the call, got their advice, thanked them and was ready to say goodbye after 9 minutes and 55 seconds.

Now, at that point, out of politeness and gratitude, I said, "I'm conscious we agreed 10 minutes", but to my surprise that person responded with, "It's OK, I've got a few minutes before my next call". In hindsight, I thought I understood what they were doing with the whole 10-minute thing. They were giving themselves a 'get out' if they needed it and made sure the caller got to the point quickly. It was a masterclass in influencing others to respect their time, and when I had an almost identical experience with someone else at a later date, it absolutely reinforced to me that it was very much a deliberate thing that these successful people were doing.

Quality of time over quantity of time – every time.

Level Five

Block 14

Freedom

When I speak to people about their goals in life and business, they usually have one thing in common. There are undoubtedly thousands of different things that people want in their life, but they all seem to have a common thread running through them.

In one way or another, the thing that everyone wants is freedom. The financial freedom to be able to afford the things they want in life, the time freedom to be able to do all the things they want without having to ask for permission, and the health freedom to be physically able to enjoy it all with the people they love.

Freedom for the next thing

There are countless examples of people who achieve their goal only to find that it didn't give them the happiness and fulfilment that they thought it would. Lottery winners can easily fall into an unfamiliar lifestyle of temptation and suspicion. Olympic gold medal winners can achieve the dream that they've worked so hard for, but soon find themselves experiencing post-gold blues.

When people retire, they can feel lost. They've suddenly got the time for all the things they want to do, but somehow they can't bring themselves to actually do them.

Why does this happen? It often seems as though the journey is more important than the destination. In other words, it seems that the thrill of the chase is so exciting that the kill can only ever be an anti-climax. When people talk about their greatest achievements, they normally talk about how it felt to *do* them rather than how it feels to have actually *done* them. Listen out for it next time you're watching or listening to a keynote, after dinner speech or a TED Talk.

It's crazy to think that something as positive as achieving your goals can have a negative side to it, but just as the old saying goes, 'every cloud has a silver lining', it seems that every silver lining can also have a cloud.

Whether it's money, an important role, or a material possession to strive for, when it's suddenly real, people can lose the purpose and focus they need to drive them forwards. For that reason, it is important to always have new goals. When you achieve one thing, enjoy your success and swiftly move to the next thing. The next goal might be to do a similar thing again but better, or it may be something completely different. It doesn't really matter as long as it is meaningful enough for you to strive for it.

Freedom within

Lots of goals involve extrinsic things like money, trophies, big houses and flashy cars.

Although these things can be powerful motivators, nothing can compare to the intrinsic feelings of happiness, contentment and fulfilment. I think this poem by G. Moriarty entitled, 'The Road Ahead or The Road Behind' nicely sums this up:

Sometimes I think the Fates must grin, as we denounce them and insist, the only reason we can't win, is the Fates themselves that miss.

Yet there lives on the ancient claim: we win or lose within ourselves. The shining trophies on our shelves, can never win tomorrow's game.

You and I know deeper down there's always a chance to win the crown; but when we fail to give our best, we simply haven't met the test, of giving all and saving none, until the game is really won.

Of showing what is meant by grit, of playing through when others quit; of playing through not letting up, it's bearing down that wins the cup.

Of dreaming there's a goal ahead, of hoping when our dreams are dead, of praying when our hopes have fled, yet losing, not afraid to fall, if bravely we have given all.

For who can ask more of a man, that giving all within his span. Giving all it seems to me, is not so far from victory.

And so the fates are seldom wrong, no matter how they twist and wind, it's you and I who make our fates — we open up or close the gates, on the road ahead or the road behind".

You will probably find that true freedom will consist of both intrinsic and extrinsic elements. You'll need to have enough money to fund the lifestyle you want, and you'll need to acquire it without eating into too much of the time you want to spend doing the things that make you truly happy.

You'll also need to feel as though you've made - and continue to make - a difference; in your life, in your business, in the world. When you have all of these things, you will probably consider yourself to have achieved freedom and mastered your time.

If you're like me, the more you think about it, the more it may become clear to you that it isn't the achievement of the goal itself that is the most important thing. It's about what you become in the process of chasing it.

By mastering your time, you will achieve many victories and enjoy the rewards that they bring, but that isn't the biggest benefit to all of this. The greater benefit is the process of strengthening every block in your time pyramid to make the best use of the time you have and become the best possible version of yourself.

The best version of you will be great to see. When others see you they will be inspired to become the best version of themselves, too. And if everyone was the best version of themselves, the world would be a better place.

Now, don't you think it's about time?